WASHINGTON'S
HISTORY

Work crew, Grand Coulee Dam, late 1930s.

WestWinds
Press
Pocket Guide

WASHINGTON'S HISTORY

The People, Land, and Events
of the Far Northwest

REVISED EDITION

HARRY RITTER

WESTWINDS
PRESS®

Revised Edition first printed in 2018

Library of Congress Cataloging-in-Publication Data

Names: Ritter, Harry, author.
Title: Washington's history : the people, land, and events of the far
    Northwest / Harry Ritter.
Description: Revised edition. | Berkeley, CA : WestWinds Press, an
    imprint of Graphic Arts Books, [2018] | Includes index.
Identifiers: LCCN 2018028689 (print) | LCCN 2018030723 (ebook) |
    ISBN 9781513261782 (ebook) | ISBN 9781513261690 (pbk.) |
    ISBN 9781513261775 (hardcover)
Subjects: LCSH: Washington (State)--History. | Natural history--
    Washington (State)
Classification: LCC F891 (ebook) | LCC F891 .R58 2018 (print) |
    DDC 979.7--dc23
LC record available at https://lccn.loc.gov/2018028689

Cartographer: Gray Mouse Graphics
Index: Sheila Ryan

Cover image: Pierre Leclerc/Shutterstock.com

Proudly distributed by Ingram Publisher Services.

Printed in the U.S.A.

WestWinds Press®
is an imprint of

GRAPHIC ARTS
BOOKS®

GraphicArtsBooks.com

GRAPHIC ARTS BOOKS
Publishing Director: Jennifer Newens
Marketing Manager: Angela Zbornik
Editor: Olivia Ngai
Design & Production: Rachel Lopez Metzger

CONTENTS

Women hikers along Middle Fork Trail, Cascade Mountains, about 1910.

THE TWENTIETH CENTURY AND BEYOND

The romance of flight, Graham's Airfield, Bellingham, 1928.

ACKNOWLEDGMENTS

I am grateful to many people for helping bring this book to publication. Ellen Wheat, formerly with Graphic Arts Center Publishing Company, first suggested that I write a short history of Washington state. Tricia Brown was my kind editorial liaison with Graphic Arts and made crucial suggestions for trimming the book's first draft. Don Graydon read the entire text in its final stages and helped bring clarity and precision to the manuscript. Special help in finding pictures for the book was supplied by Tammy Belts of Wilson Library's Special Collections Division at Western Washington University, Jeff Jewell of the Whatcom Museum of History and Art, Judy Quill of the Grand Coulee Dam photo archives, Mike Vouri of San Juan Island National Historical Park, Gary K. Miller of Energy Northwest, and Kirk Rudy of the Edward S. Curtis Gallery, McCloud, California. I also wish to thank Lisa Pirkkala of the Spokane House Interpretive Center, Joshua Binus of Fort Vancouver National Historic Site, my friends and neighbors Catherine and Bill Ouweneel, my colleague Marc Richards, and Marilyn Darke and Gary Busselman of the Columbia River Exhibition of History, Science, and Technology in Richland.

Lastly I wish to thank my wife Marian, my son Alan, and my sister Gloria for their support and encouragement.

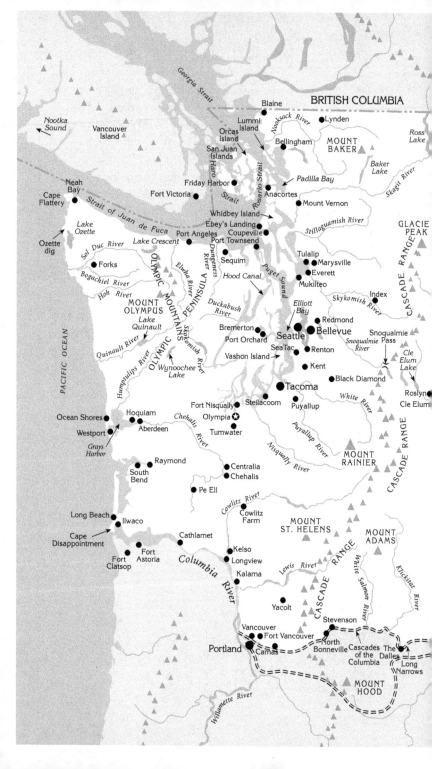

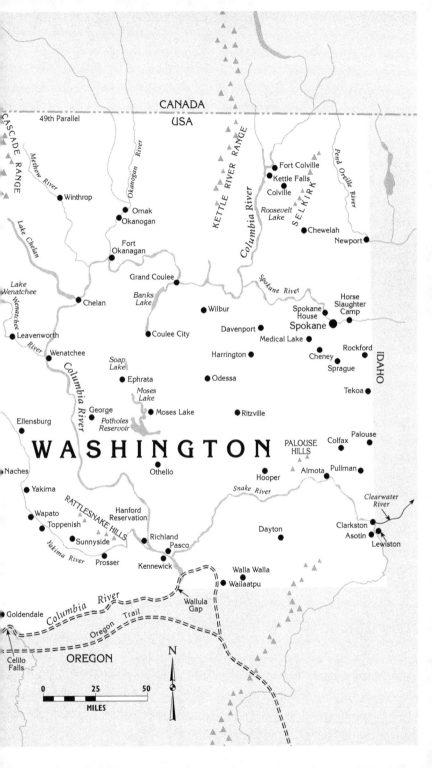

Preface to the Second Edition

I wish to thank Jennifer Newens and the Ingram Content Group for inviting me to prepare a second edition of *Washington's History*. I'm delighted that the first edition's success warrants a revision and updates. The book's small, take-it-with-you format, retained here and originally suggested for its first edition by Ellen Wheat of Westwinds Press, presents the author with some special and rewarding challenges. Divided into short essays or "chapters" limited to two facing pages, it requires the author to reduce sweeping, multilayered topics to some meaningful aspect of the gist of things. Trying to find the right word and organizing conception is truly an exciting adventure.

It is no exaggeration to say that in the past fifteen years, since the first edition's appearance, some dramatic changes have occurred in Washington State, and I have added three new chapters on Amazon, Starbucks, and Artificial Intelligence research to discuss these developments. I've also added a new postscript. Where needed, I have made changes and updates throughout the text—as, for instance, in the essays on the Kennewick Man archaeological find and the Hanford Reservation clean-up problem. As in the first edition, I want to thank my wife Marian for her encouragement and suggestions in preparing this second edition, and I also want to credit Bill Frier for a valuable tip about an information source and Geoff Middaugh for permission to use a quotation.

PROLOGUE:
THE NORTHWEST
OF THE IMAGINATION

Mount Baker and Cascade Range from Whidbey Island by John Mix Stanley, 1853.

FUTURES PAST

Near the mouth of Whatcom Creek, Bellingham Bay, about 1885.

"The past is a foreign country," novelist L. P. Hartley once wrote. "They do things differently there."

They not only do things differently, they think otherwise as well. Gazing south in 1868 from Whatcom Creek on Bellingham Bay, Victorian artist Edmund T. Coleman pondered the vista with painterly flair. "When standing here at early morn," he mused, "looking out upon the tranquil scene, in the distance the Olympian Mountains bathed in mist, and nearer the grand outline of Orcas Island looming up like some great fortification, imagination pictures the future . . . When these silent shores shall be lined with wharves and resonant with the throng of busy multitudes."

Such fancies arouse mixed emotions today, when we sometimes fret over too many people and too much growth. They were common among early visitors to the soil that became Washington state in 1889. Newcomers imagined the Northwest as a fresh tablet, ready for new inscriptions. Theirs was an age of great expectations and new beginnings, but their minds were furnished with notions inspired by European and East Coast experiences. For Coleman, Whatcom Creek was like a Welsh mountain stream. A glacial valley he viewed from Mount Baker "wanted only a 'chalet' or two, a flock of goats descending the hill-side, with the sound of tinkling bells, to make me believe that I was in Switzerland." The Lummi and Nooksack Indians' belief in forest spirits reminded him of German folktales. It's difficult to say how early Indians imagined their own landscape, or their first encounters with aliens like Coleman. Missionaries were already working to change things, but Indian minds in the mid-1800s were furnished differently from those of newcomers—and even from those of today's Native Americans.

History includes changes that occur inside people's minds over time, as well as actions and events. This book aims to supply a compact and readable account of Washington's history, revolving around changing visions of its regions and its pasts and futures. Those visions have wrought stunning improvements but also unexpected consequences. One thinks of epidemics among the Indians, inadvertently introduced by settlers who envisioned a promised land in bloom; of engineering the wild Columbia to (in Woody Guthrie's words) "turn darkness into dawn," and of destroying fisheries in the process; of the Hanford project, whose plutonium helped win World War II but whose toxins remain. Pondering those imaginings and their results is instructive, often exciting, and always interesting.

Twenty years after Coleman imagined the future, on the eve of Washington's statehood, naturalist John Muir could still write: "To many, especially in the Atlantic States, Washington . . . is regarded as being yet a far wild west—a dim, nebulous expanse of woods." Those people, Muir declared, "do not know that railroads and steamers have brought the country out of the wilderness and abolished the old distances. It is now near to all the world and is in possession of a share of the best of all that civilization has to offer, while on some of the lines of advancement it is at the front."

A few years later, the discovery of Klondike gold made Seattle the staging point for the Yukon and Alaska gold rushes, catapulting Washington from the frontier to the modern era. Another strand of our story extends Muir's thoughts on "advancement." It traces the way Washington moved in 100 years from the world's margins to a front-and-center spot in the global age of Boeing and Microsoft.

BEGINNINGS

Columbia River south of Kennewick, Washington.

Police assumed the bones were those of a drowning or homicide victim. In July 1996, two young men stumbled upon a human skeleton while watching hydroplane races on the Columbia River at Kennewick, Washington. Their discovery threw hallowed beliefs about Washington's prehistory into question, and sparked a legal battle that captured headlines.

James Chatters, a forensic anthropologist, examined the remains at the coroner's request, deciding they belonged to a white male, forty to fifty-five years of age. He thought the bones were old—possibly from the 1800s. When he sent a fragment to a radiocarbon lab for dating, the report came back: the scrap was 9,200 to 9,500 years old—among the oldest found in North America.

Further study showed that the skull of Kennewick Man—as Chatters dubbed the remains—didn't exhibit the structure associated with modern Native Americans. He thought it was Caucasoid—European-like—and some archaeologists speculated it belonged to a non-Indian group that might have reached America even before Indians arrived. But then a coalition of Indian tribes demanded the bones for burial under the Native American Graves Protection and Repatriation Act. The federal law was enacted in 1990 to ensure the return of Indian remains collected by museums in the 1800s, as well as Native ownership of newly discovered Indian remains.

Tribal leaders didn't buy Chatters's theory that the relics were non-Indian. They argued that Indians had lived on the Columbia from time immemorial. Perhaps Techamnish Oytpamanat—the

Ancient One, as they called him—was just an Indian whose bones didn't match modern stereotypes. Government officials agreed, and prepared to give the skeleton to the tribes. But eight prominent scholars filed suit in federal court to block the turnover, arguing it would violate science's right to inquiry. A media bonfire ensued, which pitted science against Indian lore.

The debate revealed that the prehistory of Washington—and of the Americas—is shrouded in uncertainty. For decades, scholars agreed that the New World's first inhabitants were the ancestors of today's Indians. These Paleo-Americans were Asian hunters, so the theory went, who came in a series of migrations via a land bridge that once connected Siberia and Alaska. When the last ice age ended about 12,000 years ago, sea levels rose and the bridge was submerged. Some hunters then roamed south through ice-free corridors that opened up along the Rockies, becoming the ancestors of all Indians of North and South America.

But recent discoveries suggest that some migrants may have paddled south in boats even earlier, along the Northwest coast, as glaciers receded into fjords. Were they related to today's Indians? The first trace of humans in today's Washington is the Manis site near Sequim, where radiocarbon tests suggest that mastodon bones mingled with spear points may be 12,000 years old. Artifacts at other Washington digs are thought to be 9,000 to 10,000 years old. Yet at some of these sites there is nothing to suggest cultural affiliation with modern Indians, and controversies like those over Kennewick Man highlight our meager understanding of how America was first peopled.

While the scientists' case was before federal court, the bones were locked up at Seattle's Burke Museum. Without further study they could not be plausibly linked to any group. A 2004 court decision allowed scientists to examine the remains and initially it seemed they might not be Native American. Later tests with new DNA technology, however, suggested the opposite. As a result, Congress awarded the remains to the tribes, and Native leaders buried them at a secret site in early 2017. At least one chapter in the cloudy history of Washington's remote past was laid to rest.

Tlakliut Indian rock paintings, Wishram, Washington.

NATIVE
CULTURES

INDIANS OF THE PLATEAU

LEFT: *Yakima fishermen, Celilo Falls, 1956, before falls were flooded by dams.*
RIGHT: *"She Who Watches," Indian rock painting on Columbia River.*

The Indians who settled Washington's interior, east of the Cascade Mountains, were part of the Plateau Culture. Their home was the district drained by the Columbia and Snake River systems. Their descendants include the Yakima, Wishram, Spokane, Nez Perce, Cayuse, and many others. When Lewis and Clark visited in 1805–6, they found scores of Plateau communities. In winter, Plateau people clustered at river junctions in villages of pit houses and tule reed lodges.

The Plateau is an arid steppe pierced by large gullies—known as coulees—and basalt cliffs sculpted by ice-age floods. (Some regional terms come from the French of early trappers; *coulée* means flowing—by extension, a ravine cut by flowing water.) At higher elevations, the scablands are skirted by stands of ponderosa pine. In the southeast are the bunchgrass hills of the Palouse (*pelouse* is French for "grass land") and the fir and spruce forests of the Blue Mountains. Summer days may exceed 100ºF and winter temperatures can dip far below zero. Precipitation varies, but at lower levels it is under ten inches a year.

But the land's severity was tempered by the yearly return of salmon from the Pacific to spawning beds as far inland as Idaho's Redfish Lake. For the Indians, hunting, trapping, and root gathering augmented the annual salmon harvest. Roots were as readily available as salmon and just as important to the diet. Bitterroot, the first to ripen, was dug by women in the spring. In early summer, women harvested camas root, similar to onion. In late summer, people moved higher up, to hunt deer and gather berries in the Okanagan uplands and Blue Mountains.

The Dalles (French for "flat stones" or "flat rock rapids"), below Celilo Falls, was the "great emporium or mart of the Columbia," according to fur trader Alexander Ross. Thousands of Plateau Indians gathered there in spring and summer to fish, trade, gamble, and socialize. Like other sacred river sites, it is still watched over by paintings and carvings they left in the basalt. Plateau people devised effective ways to catch and conserve the salmon, using weirs and netting or spearing the fish from platforms positioned above rough water, where the fish gathered strength before leaping upstream. The dry climate was a blessing, enabling women to cure fish on vast open-air racks. Lewis and Clark reckoned 30,000 pounds were dried at The Dalles.

Salmon were vital to Plateau life, but around 1730 the fishing culture was amplified by the Spanish horse, obtained via Ute middlemen from New Mexico. Yakima, Cayuse, and Walla Walla traders then opened trade routes to California, where they got more. The horse's influence was akin to the Model T's impact on American lives in the 1920s. Horses flourished on the Plateau, becoming a new form of wealth that sparked the beginnings of an equestrian social hierarchy. Lewis and Clark described vast herds, and some rich families amassed 1,000 head or more.

The Nez Perce bred the Appaloosa (palouse horse), and the Cayuse were such famed breeders that their name was synonymous with the Indian pony. The mobility of horses allowed some groups, like the Nez Perce, to make buffalo-hunting forays east of the Rockies. Such changes led to wider intertribal alliances, and defensive wars against Plains and Great Basin confederations—the Blackfoot, the Shoshone, the Paiute—who used horses and firearms to expand their power. Plateau people maintained traditional trading and marriage ties to saltwater people of the Pacific Coast, but with the horse's arrival they also adopted many features of Plains Indian life—hide tepees, beaded buckskin clothing, braided hair, and feathered headdresses. Thus, at the time of European contact in the late 1700s, Plateau cultures were in the midst of change.

INDIANS OF THE COAST

Makah whalers off Washington Coast, about 1930. Asahel Curtis photo.

The Indians who moved from Washington's Plateau to its Pacific shore, starting perhaps 8,000 years ago, evolved into the Northwest Coast Culture. They shared similarities in technology and belief that sprang from their forest and saltwater world. From the Chinook at the Columbia's mouth, north to the Lummi on Georgia Strait, they enjoyed a mild climate, plentiful food, and abundant wood for houses and tools. Fishing in spring and summer, supplemented by forest hunting and gathering, supplied most of the year's food. Their *middens*—kitchen dumps of coastal communities—testify to the role of shellfish in their diet. One Snohomish delta mound stands six feet high and extends a quarter-mile. The Makah of Neah Bay on the Olympic Peninsula made a specialty of whaling, and recent efforts by some of their members to revive the whaling tradition have aroused world controversy.

The key ingredients in coastal life were salmon and red cedar. Salmon, returning in yearly rhythms, permitted relative affluence. In annual rituals, Coast people gave thanks—like Plateau Indians— for the year's first returning fish. From cedar, saltwater people derived rot-resistant wood for tools; planks for post-and-beam houses; bark, branches, and roots for ropes, fishnets, and clothing;

and logs for canoes. They devised effective ways of working the aromatic wood. Two men could fell a forest giant in three days, using controlled fire, stone chisels, and bone wedges. Canoe-makers crafted seaworthy vessels by hollowing logs with adzes and fire, then widening the cavity with water heated by hot stones. Women pounded the inner bark, weaving it into baskets, skirts, and rain-shedding hats and capes.

Nature's generosity permitted leisure—at least for privileged classes—which coastal people used to develop rituals and kinship systems. Wealth was important, with society divided into hierarchies of nobles, commoners, and slaves. Adept at commerce, some groups—like the Chinook—were famous as brokers. After European contact, a trading language of Native and European words—"Chinook jargon"—evolved to facilitate exchange.

A defining tradition was the potlatch, a feast involving dancing, gambling, and gift-giving. Potlatches were held to mark major events such as births and marriages and to validate the status of the hosts. The more wealth a leader gave away, the more prestige he earned. Wood carving flourished, and coastal artists evolved a distinctive style revolving around totemic motifs. The carvings were painted in red and black pigments derived from clay, charcoal, and other natural materials, with masticated salmon eggs as a binder. But Washington's coastal Indians did not carve the freestanding totem poles created by their northern cultural relatives of British Columbia and Alaska.

It's tempting for modern minds to romanticize the coastal way of life, but it was not really Eden. Puget Sound Indians feared raids by more warlike groups to the north—the Kwakiutl and Haida of today's Canada. There were lean as well as fat years, and some villages controlled richer harvest grounds than others. Coast societies were ruled by wealthy elites, they were often at war, and slavery was widely practiced. Slaves—captured in war or purchased from other tribes—were commodities and might be put to death by their masters. Unless set free, their condition was hereditary. Still, Coast Native traditions exert a persistent appeal: twentieth-century Washington botanist Arthur Kruckeberg believed the coastal life "had the potential for self-perpetuation in a land of natural self-restoring abundance."

EUROPEAN CONTACT AND ITS IMPACT

Tomb of Chinook Chief Concomly, victim of the "fever and ague" in 1830. Engraving made in 1841.

The encounter of Northwest Indians and outsiders, starting in the 1770s, was fateful for the region that became Washington. Initial meetings occurred on fairly equal terms. The earliest newcomers were explorers and traders who were confident in their technical skills and imagined superiority but nonetheless curious about the customs of aboriginal people. They knew they were outnumbered intruders in a strange land. The Indians who met them were at home and secure in their relationship to their land and traditions. They were curious, as well, about the aliens.

The outsiders came to trade, and Natives were expert traders, eager for things the strangers brought: iron chisels and cooking pots; woolen blankets; rum and tobacco; firearms; and beads and jackets for adornment. Europeans were surprised by the Natives' business acumen. Their sense of supply and demand had been honed by experience in trade networks that stretched from the Columbia to Alaska, the Great Plains, and California. Trader Richard Cleveland wrote that "the Indians are sufficiently cunning to derive all possible advantage from competition . . . Showing themselves to be [as] well versed in the tricks of the trade as the greatest adepts." That the intruders were keen for the skins of common animals—the sea otter and beaver—was as amusing to Natives as their own yen for beads—especially blue ones—was to Europeans.

Yet the downside for Natives was swiftly revealed. Rum was a scourge, and firearms nourished lethal conflict among Indians themselves. Worst of all were diseases for which they had no immunity: measles, influenza, typhus—and above all, smallpox. In 1774, when the Spanish ship *Santiago* under Juan Perez called at the Queen Charlotte Islands and Nootka Sound, perhaps 200,000 people lived on the coast between Oregon and Alaska. Perez bartered with Indian traders, and in 1775 a second Spanish expedition arrived under Captains Heceta and Bodega y Quadra. The first smallpox outbreak, which raged in the mid-1770s, probably sprang from these encounters. Before running its course, it claimed a third of the people along the coast, and infected Plateau Indians as well. Smallpox erupted again in 1801, and Lewis and Clark recorded the scarred faces of survivors they met in 1805.

An outbreak of smallpox, or perhaps measles, called "the mortality," swept through the Coast and Plateau in 1824 and 1825, when 10 to 20 percent of the Native population perished. Then came the "fever and ague"—probably malaria or influenza—carried to the Columbia by the American ships *Convoy* and *Owyhee*, which anchored at Fort Vancouver in 1830. Dr. John McLoughlin, head of the post, reckoned that three-quarters of local Natives perished. Death paid a return visit each year in the 1830s. Sadly, the Native remedy of steaming in sweat lodges, then plunging in cold water, made things worse. The Chinook, who once controlled trade in the area, were decimated.

Missionaries and settlers began to arrive in the 1830s and 1840s, via the Oregon Trail. They brought typhus, measles, and dysentery. By this time, the waves of death had sapped Natives' numbers and their ability to resist white settlement on their land. Slowly, Native immunity built up, and vaccines became available. The last epidemics in the Northwest occurred in 1862–63, 1868, and 1874. Yet, according to some estimates, in the century between then and that first Spanish visit in 1774, the coastal Native population plunged 80 percent, and that of the Plateau was cut in half.

Entrance to the Strait of John de Fuca from Voyages by John Meares, 1790.

MARITIME AND OVERLAND EXPLORATION OF THE NORTHWEST

Spanish and Russian Incursions

Construction of the Spanish palisade at Núñez Gaona (Neah Bay), 1792,
first European settlement in the future Washington, by José Cardero.

Between 1492 and 1792—from the voyage of Columbus to that of
George Vancouver—navigators revolutionized Europe's knowledge
of the globe. The Americas were discovered, the coasts of Africa
were mapped, the Pacific was explored. America's Northwest was last
to fall under the European eye. For most of that span, Spain was the
reigning sea power. In 1513, Balboa sighted the Pacific from Panama,
claiming "any coasts that it might wash" for Spain. The ocean's
reputation as a Spanish lake was bolstered by the conquest of the
Philippines in the 1560s. With Mexico, Peru, and Asia at its feet,
Spain displayed scant interest in the north Pacific.

Spain's involvement in northern latitudes was only aroused by
Russian intrusions in Alaska. In 1728, Vitus Bering probed the sea
between Siberia and America, now called the Bering Strait. In 1741
he made another voyage, landing in southern Alaska and
establishing Russia's claim. His crew returned with news that
Alaskan waters teemed with sea otter, the plushest of furs,
commanding fabulous prices in China. Siberian hunters scrambled

to exploit the wealth, and by the 1780s Russia controlled the world's richest fur trade. Grigori Shelikov created the Russian-American Company and founded the Northwest's first permanent European settlement, on Kodiak Island in 1784. In 1799 Tsar Paul I awarded the firm a monopoly on the Alaska trade, and in 1808, company manager Alexander Baranov moved its headquarters to Sitka. Under Baranov, the company hunted otter as far south as Washington and even California.

Russia shrouded its actions in secrecy, but news leaked out and Spain sent ships north to assert its claims. In 1774, Juan Perez sailed as far north as the Queen Charlotte Islands and Nootka Sound on Vancouver Island's outer coast. He reached a latitude of 54° 40' N, a feat that ironically became grounds for later U.S. claims to the coast (and the slogan "Fifty-four forty or fight") after America inherited Spanish territorial claims by an 1819 treaty. In 1775, Spain dispatched another expedition, led by Bruno de Heceta and Bodega y Quadra. Heceta landed near the Quinault River on the Olympic Peninsula, claiming it for Spain. His sketch is the first known chart of Washington's coast, but some of Bodega's men were killed by Indians when they went ashore for water—an ill omen of Spain's future in the region. Sailing south, Heceta encountered powerful tides at the entrance to an inlet, which he thought might be "the mouth of some great river or some passage to another sea." It was the Columbia, but his crew was ravaged by scurvy and he couldn't enter its mouth.

In 1790, Spanish navigators Manuel Quimper and López de Haro made a circuit of Juan de Fuca Strait, claiming Neah Bay for Spain, reaching Puget Sound's entrance, and discerning on the northeast horizon today's Mount Baker. But it was Francisco de Eliza who made the best Spanish survey of Washington's inside seas. Sailing south from Nootka, Eliza charted the San Juan Archipelago between May and August, 1791, leaving names that endure on today's charts: *Canal de Nuestra Señora del Rosario* (Rosario Strait), *Seno de Padilla* (Padilla Bay), and *Isla y Archipelago de San Juan*—the San Juan Islands themselves. Departing from its previous policy of secrecy, Spain made Eliza's charts available to Britain, and they were useful in Vancouver's exploration of the region in 1792.

In the Golden Hind's Wake

Francis Drake (left) and Capt. James Cook.

James Cook was Britain's greatest explorer, and his third voyage of discovery, undertaken in 1776–80, centered on the Northwest coast. Cook's orders were to determine, once and for all, if a Northwest Passage connected the Atlantic and Pacific. From the 1560s onward, a hypothetical Strait of Anían—a nautical equivalent of El Dorado— tantalized navigators. Should such a waterway exist, it would be a shortcut to the China trade.

Cook was not the first Englishman to sail the Pacific or seek the fabled strait. In Shakespeare's day, Elizabethan sea dog Francis Drake circled the globe. He sailed up the coasts of Chile and Mexico in 1578 and 1579, looting Spanish galleons. Then he headed north, hoping to return to London by a Northwest Passage. In 1579 he may have reached 48° N, near Cape Flattery on Washington's Olympic Peninsula. Here, according to an account published after his death, he decided there was no passage.

Centuries later, in the 1970s, archeologists found brass tacks at the peninsula's Ozette dig, fueling conjecture that they came from Drake's ship, the *Golden Hind*. But they might have come from a Spanish galleon, blown off course on its return from the Philippines. Drake did repair the *Hind* in a bay, most likely on today's Oregon or California coast. He mapped the inlet, naming it *Portus Nova Albionis* and claiming it for Queen Elizabeth. Thereafter, New

Albion appeared often on atlases—anywhere from today's California to Alaska. Despite Drake's exploits, England's awareness of the region remained a matter of fantasy. It took Captain Cook to change that.

Cook's life was a far cry from Drake's checkered career. A man of science, he sailed north from Hawaii in 1778. After five weeks he sighted—with homage to Drake—"the long lost coast of New Albion" at Yaquina Bay (present-day Oregon). Among his officers were William Bligh—of later "mutiny on the *Bounty*" notoriety—and midshipman George Vancouver, Cook's successor as a Northwest explorer. In the *Resolution* and the *Discovery* the expedition proceeded north, missing the Columbia and Juan de Fuca Strait. He did spot and name Cape Flattery at the strait's entrance, however, on March 22, 1778. At Nootka Sound on Vancouver Island's outer coast (already discovered by Spain's Juan Perez), Cook paused to rerig his vessels. There his men obtained sea otter pelts from Indians in return for nails and bits of iron. The sailors wanted the furs for cloaks, but when they returned to England in 1780, via Canton, they discovered that otter pelts brought astronomical prices in China. Their reports brought scores of British and New England traders to the Northwest coast, once the American Revolutionary War ended in 1783. It was the first chapter in opening Washington's coast and Columbia Basin to British and Yankee commerce.

Meanwhile, back in 1778, Cook weighed anchor and continued north. He reached Alaska, found Cook's Inlet (site of modern Anchorage), and sailed through the Bering Strait, halting at 70° N when confronted by pack ice. He had proven that Asia and America were not joined. Still, the legend of the Northwest Passage was not laid to rest, since storms kept him offshore during his journey up the coast. He planned to return the following year to settle the matter, but the season was late and he turned south, to winter and replenish his stores. In February 1779, before completing his quest, the great navigator was killed by Polynesian warriors at Kalakaua Bay, in a dispute over a stolen boat on Hawaii's Big Island.

From Nootka to Puget Sound

Mount Rainier from the south part of Admiralty Inlet, by J. Sykes, 1792.
From Vancouver's Voyage.

The greatest alumnus of Captain Cook's last voyage was George Vancouver. A midshipman under Cook, Vancouver returned to the Pacific in 1792 as master of Cook's ship, the *Discovery*, with orders to make one last search for the Northwest Passage. When the task was finished in 1795, it proved the passage was a myth and yielded the 18th century's best survey of the channels that stretch from Puget Sound to Alaska. Vancouver had another mission, as well. He was to meet Spanish commandant Bodega y Quadra at Nootka Sound. They were to finalize a treaty signed in 1790, to resolve the Nootka Controversy.

The Nootka dispute had nudged England and Spain to the brink of war in 1789, and its resolution had implications for Washington's future. Following Cook's visit in 1778, Nootka Sound on Vancouver Island became a hub of the sea otter trade. British and Boston merchantmen swarmed to the spot. Spain, worried by Russian expansion in Alaska, now perceived a more serious British challenge—especially after Englishman John Meares erected a trading post in the Sound in 1788. In response, Spain dispatched an ill-tempered captain named Esteban José Martínez in 1789. Martínez constructed his own outpost and arrested two of Meares's associates, commandeering their ships and sending the two men to Mexico in chains. England seized on the incident as a pretext to pry open Spain's Pacific realm to British trade. England threatened war and Spain's ally, France, was paralyzed by the start of its famous revolution in May 1789—the very month of Martínez's blunder. In 1790, Spain signed a treaty recognizing Britain's right to trade in Northwest waters.

Vancouver arrived in April 1792, to seal the agreement and start his exploration. Before his rendezvous with Bodega y Quadra, he cruised Washington's coast. Like Cook, he missed the Columbia's mouth, obscured by breakers on its bar. Only two days later, on April 28, he met Boston trader Robert Gray, sailing south. On May 12, Gray found the river and negotiated its entrance in his ship *Columbia Rediviva*, naming it Columbia's River—thus establishing America's prior claim to it and its watershed. When Vancouver heard of Gray's feat later that summer, he sent Lt. William Broughton in the *Chatham* into the river as far as present-day Portland, sowing the seed of future British-American conflict.

Vancouver had missed the Columbia, but he didn't miss the Strait of Juan de Fuca (already discovered by Charles Barkley in 1787). On the day after his encounter with Gray, he marveled as he gazed toward a vista bounded by Mount Baker and Mount Rainier—both of which he named (Baker after one of his officers, Rainier after a British admiral). It was a panorama, he enthused, "almost as enchantingly beautiful as the most elegantly finished pleasure grounds in Europe." Vancouver spent two months charting Washington's inland seas, and today's charts brim with names he and his crewmen bestowed: Puget's Sound, Hood's Canal, Admiralty Inlet, Whidbey Island, Deception Pass, Bellingham Bay, and others. At Tulalip he claimed the land for King George III, christening it New Georgia—a name that one ironic day would make way for the king's nemesis, Washington.

In August 1792, Vancouver sailed north to keep his appointment with Bodega y Quadra. The meeting was cordial, and England had achieved its goal of penetrating the Pacific trade. Spain and England even shared charts, and began to coordinate their surveys. A sea change had occurred. Spain's tide in the Pacific ebbed, that of Britain and America was on the rise.

LEWIS AND CLARK

Meriwether Lewis (left) and William Clark.

On August 13, 1805, in the Bitterroot Mountains of today's Idaho, Captain Meriwether Lewis relished the taste of baked salmon, given to him by Shoshone Indians. "This was the first salmon I had seen," he recorded, "and [it] perfectly convinced me that we were on the waters of the Pacific Ocean." Fifteen months earlier, he and fellow Virginian William Clark had departed St. Louis. They led the Corps of Discovery of forty-five men, authorized by President Jefferson to explore America's Louisiana Purchase, and beyond. They were to find "the most direct & practicable water communication across this continent for the purposes of commerce."

The thought of reaching the Columbia's mouth buoyed the men's spirits, for they had misjudged the journey. Departing Fort Mandan in March 1805, Lewis thought the portage from the Missouri's headwaters to the Columbia would require "half a days march." Yet crossing the Continental Divide took weeks, and the explorers nearly starved. Sadly, Lewis concluded that finding an easy river passage to the Pacific—the point of their trek—was an illusion.

The explorers were also surprised by the Snake and Columbia Rivers. They expected the continent's western watershed to mirror its east side, imagining terrain that sloped to the sea. Instead they found a landscape of extremes. Descending the Snake's towering canyons and white water, they emerged to the glare of sagebrush desert—"open country," in Clark's words, "where the eye has no rest." Impatient to reach the sea, the explorers grew irritable. Lewis, prone to melancholy, ceased making journal entries. The men survived on dog meat, acquired by trade with Plateau Indians. Salmon were everywhere, but it was October, they had spawned, and their carcasses were decaying in streams. To the Indians' amazement the explorers refused offers of dried fish, fearing it was tainted.

The Columbia was a greater adversary than the meandering Missouri. At points, it fell in thundering cataracts. The river's Long Narrows were, for Clark, an "agitated gut swelling boiling & whorling in every direction." Negotiating the Columbia Gorge, they passed from arid steppe into emerald forest, where rainfall averaged seventy inches. The river broadened and on November 6, Clark proclaimed "*Ocian in view!* O! The joy." Jubilation was premature, however, for the weather turned foul, pinning them down on stony beaches and drenching them with rain. It was mid-November before they rounded Washington's southwest tip at Cape Disappointment and carved their names in trees, with Clark adding "By Land from the U. States in 1804 & 1805."

The soldiers built a winter camp near the Columbia's south shore, christened Fort Clatsop. Elk were plentiful and the men ate so much elk meat over the next four months that they declared they preferred dog. Forced to await spring to make the return over the Rockies, they huddled in dank quarters. Lewis fleshed out his journals and Clark began a map of the West. The Corps returned to St. Louis on September 23, 1806, after two and one-half years and 8,000 miles of travel. One of history's great adventures, it had a somber epilogue. Lewis became governor of Louisiana in 1807, but though a superb explorer, he was no politician. He amassed debts, drank, and took medicines laced with opium and morphine. A manic-depressive in today's terms, he succumbed to despair. On October 11, 1809, bound east to arrange publication of the expedition's journals, he died of a self-inflicted pistol shot at Grinder's Inn near Nashville, Tennessee.

Sizing up the great northwest. Members of the Wilkes Expedition drawn by J. Drayton, 1841.

FUR TRADERS, PATHFINDERS, AND MISSIONARIES

THE MARITIME FUR TRADE

A sea otter, by John W. Audubon.

Spain's empire in Mexico and Peru was built on gold and silver. The world's interest in the Northwest was aroused by "soft gold"— the fur of aquatic mammals. Foremost was the sea otter. The otter's silky coat was prized above all furs on world markets. Largest of the weasels, they abounded in kelp beds of the Pacific Rim, from Japan to the Aleutians, then south to California. Without a layer of fat to protect it against frigid water, the otter evolved a lustrous coat the color of deep chocolate, unrivaled in plush density. The glossy fur was coveted by China's mandarins, and the best prices were paid at Canton. Hunting was heaviest in Alaska and Canada's coastal islands, but the otter trade left a mark on Washington's history as well.

Russian traders pioneered the maritime fur trade, monopolizing it from the 1740s to the 1780s. To harvest the pelts, Russians forced Aleut hunters into service to stalk the otters from kayaks. As hunting decimated the Alaskan otter population, Russian operations spread southward. Spain was first to learn of Russia's operations, in the late 1760s, and sent several expeditions north to block encroachment on their Pacific domain. Yet Spain's power was in eclipse, and it mounted no real effort to enter the fur trade with China.

Not so England and the United States. The word was out when Captain Cook's crew reported that otter skins commanded dazzling prices in Canton, though British and American involvement in the otter rush was delayed by the American Revolution, which ended in 1783. Then vessels were free to pursue fur riches in the Northwest. Unlike the Russians, who forced Aleut hunters to kill the otters, the English and Americans traded metal objects, beads, and muskets to the Indians, who freely collected the hides. In 1785 James Hanna was first of the "King George Men"—as Natives called the English— to visit the Northwest, in a brig aptly named the *Sea Otter*. As a prank, his men exploded gunpowder beneath the bench of Indian leader Maquinna at Nootka Sound. The chief was not amused; his warriors attacked the ship and killed several crewmen. Hanna still collected 560 pelts that fetched a handsome return in Canton.

Other traders flocked to the north Pacific in Hanna's wake. Boston merchants had special reason to venture the risk. As British colonials before 1776, their wealth revolved around the rum and slave trade with English colonies in the West Indies. After the rebellion, the Caribbean was sealed to American trade, and New England merchants thirsted for new markets. The China trade, with the otter at its apex, exercised a magnetic allure. By 1800, Yankee traders gained the upper hand over the British, bartering otter skins for China goods like tea, silk, and porcelain.

Thanks to the otter trade, many of Washington's coasts were charted. In 1787, the Englishman Charles Barkley was the first non-Native to find the Strait of Juan de Fuca. On May 12, 1792, Boston's Robert Gray entered the Columbia, establishing America's claim to the river. And Thomas Jefferson, seeking a transcontinental route to the China trade, commissioned Lewis and Clark in 1803 to scout the Northwest. In the course of it all, the otter was hunted to near extinction. It vanished from Washington's coast by around 1900, but following reintroduction in 1969 it's making a slow comeback.

THE NOR'WESTERS AND SPOKANE HOUSE

Coat of arms of the North West Company.

Sea otter pelts lured Europeans to Washington's seaboard. The region's interior was opened to commerce by an aquatic rodent, the beaver. At the dawn of white settlement, North America's river drainages supported, on average, two beavers per square mile, each animal weighing forty to seventy pounds as adults. Beavers engineered their own habitat by damming streams, creating ponds for their sapling lodges.

The demand for beavers, valued for the velvet underfur beneath their outer hairs, burgeoned when beaver-felt hats became the rage, around 1810. In eastern North America, two firms dominated the trade: England's Hudson's Bay Company and John Jacob Astor's American Fur Company. In the inland Northwest, the trade was pioneered by a rival firm, the North West Company of Montreal. In 1806 the company sent one of its partners, David Thompson, to find new trapping grounds west of the Rockies. Guided by Jacques (Jaco) Finlay, Thompson traversed the mountains in 1807 near the Columbia's headwaters in British Columbia. He mapped the river's upper regions, reached its mouth in 1811, and founded several trading posts. He hoped to build a fort at the mouth of the river, but found Astor's company already there.

Among Thompson's posts was Spokane House, constructed in 1810 by Jaco Finlay and Finan Mcdonald. The site was a pine-studded flat where the lazy Little Spokane and swifter Spokane Rivers merged, ten miles northwest of today's city of Spokane. Here, Native people—the Spokane, Coeur d'Alene, and Pend d'Oreille—met in summers to fish, gamble, and trade. Salmon, pressing upstream in their spawning odyssey, were jammed so thick that mounted fishermen waded in and lanced them from horseback. The Indians welcomed the newcomers and the goods they supplied—ironware, blankets, beads, and rum. A Native village sprang up, numbering 250 people by 1822. Trapping occurred in winter, when pelts were thickest, and most was done by company men or independent contractors—French Canadians, *métis* (men of mixed Indian and European descent), or Iroquois from the East. In 1812, the post collected 11,000 pounds of furs.

In that year Spokane House gained a rival when—a stone's throw away—Astor's company built Fort Spokane, a sturdy palisade with two bastions. The Astorians enlivened the scene: to attract Indian trade and entertain themselves, they staged dances and horse races. But Astor's firm abandoned the site after one profitable year when their main post, Fort Astoria at the Columbia's mouth, was threatened by British seizure during the War of 1812. Jaco Finlay's Nor'Westers bought their rival's more spacious quarters, which became the new Spokane House. The post flourished for a time as the launch point for expeditions into the Snake River region. The furs they collected were sent sixty miles by packhorse to the Columbia at Kettle Falls, then downriver by boat to the Pacific.

In 1821, after decades of rivalry, the North West Company and the Hudson's Bay Company combined, under the latter firm's name. By then beaver had been trapped out in the Spokane region, and company officials deserted Spokane House for a new post at Kettle Falls, christened Fort Colvile in 1826. All but Jaco Finlay went to the new post. Finlay, by now about sixty, preferred the peace of the Little Spokane. He stayed there with his Indian wife and family until he died in 1828, and was buried under the ruins of one of the old fort's bastions.

The Hudson's Bay Company

Fort Vancouver by Gustav Sohon, 1850.

The first fur company in North America, the Hudson's Bay Company, was chartered by England's Charles II in 1670. Based in London, the company was no mere business, but rather a more-or-less enlightened autocracy. With sweeping authority over Canada's wilderness, it prospered, but was challenged after 1783 by the upstart North West Company of Montreal. Competition between the firms was vicious. In 1816, Nor'Westers massacred twenty Hudson's Bay men in Manitoba. But royal pressure forced a merger of the rivals under the Hudson's Bay name in 1821, and the company extended its trapping to the Columbia River region previously controlled by the Nor'Westers.

In 1824 the company chose Quebec-born Dr. John McLoughlin to direct operations in the Columbia District. Standing six-foot-four, his mane of hair prematurely stark white, the fierce-eyed physician had a temper, iron will, and stately presence that awed Hudson's Bay employees and Natives alike. In 1825 the company built Fort Vancouver at Jolie Prairie, on the Columbia at the site of today's Vancouver, Washington. It envisioned a day when the Northwest would be divided by Britain and the United States, with the Columbia as the boundary.

The river was navigable to the fort and beyond, as far as the mouth of its gorge, and at Jolie Prairie they could raise crops and livestock to make the post self-sufficient. The Vancouver stockade was a thriving affair, its warehouses bursting with furs collected by trapping brigades from places as far-flung as Alaska and California. In 1832 the fort opened a station in Honolulu, to which it exported grain, lumber, and salted salmon. A medley of 400 to 500 souls lived in and around the Vancouver palisade—Scots, Irish, English, French Canadian, Coast Indian, Iroquois, and Kanaka (Hawaiian).

McLoughlin reigned from the whitewashed Big House, its vine-covered veranda flanked by two cannons. There he met each noon with clerks and Indian leaders while dining on blue china. Generous by nature, his wrath was fearful if aroused. Insubordination was punished by the lash. As a physician, he struggled to combat the epidemics that decimated Native people, and welcomed guests, even Americans whose permanent settlement the company tried to discourage. Narcissa Whitman, en route to her husband's mission at Waiilatpu, recalled his kindness when her party stopped at the fort.

McLoughlin's methods for harvesting beavers were disastrous. He viewed American mountain men, trapping out of St. Louis, as an avant-garde of American migration. To halt their advance, McLoughlin ordered fur brigades to comb the Rockies and Great Basin, trapping all fur-bearing species to create a "fur desert." The beaver faced extermination, but happily men's hat fashions shifted from beaver-felt to silk in the 1840s.

McLoughlin's last years were clouded by the murder of his son at Fort Stikine in Alaska, and quarrels with his superior George Simpson. In 1845 the man who tried to keep Americans out of the Northwest retired, became an American himself, and settled in the new town of Oregon City on the Willamette River. As for Fort Vancouver, after 1846 it stood in U.S. territory thanks to a treaty between England and the United States. The Hudson's Bay Company continued its operations there, but had already moved its headquarters to Fort Victoria on Canada's Vancouver Island. In 1860 the company abandoned the once-proud post on the Columbia, and it was ransacked for lumber and firewood by American colonizers. It vanished entirely, but today much of it has been marvelously reconstructed by the National Park Service.

The Astorians

Fort Okinakane (Okanagan), first American settlement in present Washington, by John Mix Stanley, 1853.

In 1810 John Jacob Astor founded the Pacific Fur Company with the aim of building a fort at the mouth of the Columbia River. Astor was a German immigrant who had already made a fortune in furs and New York real estate. The explorations of Lewis and Clark fired visions of global reach in his imagination, and from the Columbia he hoped to wrest control of the Northwest fur trade from Boston merchants and Montreal's North West Company, and monopolize commerce with China.

In 1811 Astor dispatched two parties, one by land from St. Louis and one from New York via Cape Horn and Honolulu. The naval expedition reached the Columbia first, aboard the *Tonquin* under the ironfisted command of Captain Jonathan Thorn. In April 1811 Thorn erected a trading station on the Columbia, called Fort Astoria, and then set a hasty course for Vancouver Island's west coast, to trade with Clayoquot Sound Indians. The result was one of Northwest history's bloodiest incidents, as described by its sole Astorian survivor, the Indian interpreter Lamayzie. Nursing grudges over the arrogance of previous captains, the Clayoquot were outraged when—arguing over the price of a skin—Thorn rubbed a chief's face in the pelt. Warriors boarded his ship and killed Thorn and all hands but

Lamayzie, who offered himself as a slave to Native women. Before dying, one sailor ignited the powder magazine, blowing the *Tonquin* sky-high with 200 of its attackers—"arms, legs, heads and bodies, flying in every direction," in Lamayzie's words.

Meanwhile, after a grueling overland trek, Astor's St. Louis party reached Fort Astoria in January 1812. Its head, Wilson Price Hunt, was a novice in exploration and no leader of men. The group had roamed erratically for ten months, almost starved, and had become separated several times. Crossing the badlands of today's southern Idaho, they resorted to drinking their own urine. Two men fell behind, unable to continue. They, too, reached Astoria, but only after enduring torture by Indians who then left them naked in the desert.

Despite such ordeals, a ship from New York supplied Hunt's men with trade goods and they launched a rivalry with the North West Company. Pushing east up the Columbia, they founded Fort Okanagan, the first American settlement in the future Washington. They also built Fort Spokane on the Spokane River, within eyesight of the Nor'Westers' own Spokane House. Astor's posts were better supplied than those of the Canadian firm, and they flourished for one season. But again his scheme was foiled, this time not by Indians but by foreign war. In June 1812, fighting erupted between England and the United States, and Astor's enterprise hung by a thread. England was the world's premier sea power, and it seemed only a matter of time before it seized Fort Astoria. Thus, at considerable loss, the Astorians sold their posts to the North West Company in December 1813, closing the curtain on Astor's grand design.

Yet, through Astor's reach, American claims to the region had been bolstered. Further, in the summer of 1812 a group of Astorians led by Robert Stuart had tramped overland to New York to report on the firm's progress. Following a Crow Indian trail, they found an easy way through the Rockies, over South Pass in Wyoming—essentially stumbling upon what became, in the 1840s, the route of the Oregon Trail over the continental divide.

HERALDS OF MANIFEST DESTINY

Charles Wilkes.

In the 1830s and 1840s America was gripped by a sense of manifest destiny—the notion of its God-given mission to span the continent from sea to sea. Outside of Africa and China's forbidden empire, the Northwest was one of the earth's few corners scarcely touched by European influence. Spain acknowledged its failure to rule the north Pacific in the 1790s, in the Nootka Treaty with Britain. Russia—which claimed Alaska—had neither wealth nor will to push south of latitude 54° 40'—a boundary confirmed by pacts with the United States and England in 1824 and 1825.

By the Louisiana Purchase of 1803, America owned the northern plains to the continental divide. But the wilderness west of the Rockies and north of California, then known collectively as Oregon or the Columbia District, was disputed by the U.S. and England. A handful of citizens of both nations were rivals in the otter and beaver trade, but otherwise neither country had settlers there. Thus, in an 1818 treaty, they agreed to "joint occupancy," an arrangement that lasted until 1846. This meant Britain had the initial upper hand, for London's Hudson's Bay Company—with its hub at Fort Vancouver—ruled the fur trade by the 1820s.

American senators like Missouri's Lewis Linn and Thomas Hart Benton were determined things should change. St. Louis was the staging ground for U.S. fur companies, and Linn and Benton preached westward expansion. In this climate, America's armed forces probed beyond the Mississippi, preparing for growth to the west.

In 1832, Paris-born Captain Benjamin-Louis-Eulalie de Bonneville, an army engineer trained at West Point, was granted leave—supposedly to trade furs in the Rockies. It was really a covert operation to explore the virgin West. The captain mapped wide swaths of the region, including a wagon route over Wyoming's South Pass—later the "great gate" used by pilgrims to Oregon's promised land. Bonneville was not quite the hero that Washington Irving made him seem in *The Adventures of Captain Bonneville*. But Irving's book of 1837 popularized his maps and kindled the flame of Northwest migration. (Bonneville was appointed commandant of Fort Vancouver when it became U.S. property after 1846; Bonneville Dam is named for him.) The army added to the fire with the exploits of Lt. John C. Frémont, son-in-law of Senator Benton. Heading a team of the Army Engineers, Frémont carried the banner of exploration westward, mapping the Oregon Trail in detail.

Just as important was the navy's Charles Wilkes. Between 1838 and 1842 the dashing lieutenant circled the globe with six ships. Though later court-martialed for the harsh discipline that reigned aboard his ships, Wilkes was one of the nineteenth century's great adventurers. The plant and animal specimens he collected were a cornerstone of the Smithsonian Institution, founded in 1846. After traversing Antarctic seas, he set sail for the Northwest, where he charted the Columbia's mouth, the Olympic Peninsula, and Puget Sound. Wilkes's illustrated report created the first vivid American sense of the future Washington. His key finding was that the Columbia's bar made its mouth unfit as a harbor. One of his sloops, the *Peacock*, sank trying to negotiate the barrier's raging surf and tides. The Northwest's best anchorages lay inside Puget Sound, and upon his return to New York in 1842, he urged his government to include those waters in its claims to the region. Wilkes's report caught Senator Benton's eye, and nurtured the exploits of John Frémont.

ERRAND INTO THE WILDERNESS

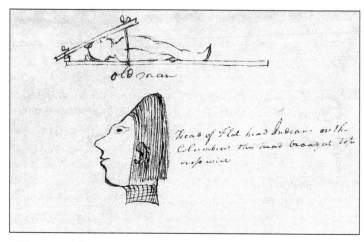

Native Head flattening, detail of sketch from William Clark's journal, 1806.

In 1833, New York newspapers ran a story that stirred eastern churches. Four Nez Perce and Flathead tribesmen, it seemed, journeyed from the Northwest to the St. Louis doorstep of William Clark, the famous explorer. Awed by the white man's power, they wished to learn his religion. The report included a drawing that showed an Indian whose forehead sloped radically backward, flattened by the pressure of a plank during infancy. Such deformation was common among Northwest tribes, who thought it flattering. East Coast Christians saw it differently—as a mark of paganism in need of redemption. The report from St. Louis put the Northwest squarely on the map of the evangelical imagination.

The Methodist Missionary Board dispatched Rev. Jason Lee and his nephew Daniel. The Lees bypassed the Nez Perce to convert Natives in the Willamette Valley. The American Missionary Board followed the Methodists' example. In 1835 it sent Samuel Parker and Marcus Whitman, a thirty-three-year-old physician from upstate New York, to scout the Northwest. Whitman returned east in 1836 to marry another apostle, Narcissa Prentiss, and the newlyweds embarked for Indian country, where they founded a mission among the Cayuse at Waiilatpu—"place of the people of the rye grass"— seven miles west of present-day Walla Walla, Washington.

Whitman was a physician, not a minister, but he embodied the Protestant ethic. With Yankee energy, he taught the Cayuse his Christian beliefs, treated their ailments, and offered himself as a role model. He made the desert bloom, creating a tidy farm watered by the Walla Walla River that flowed on the mission's south side. To redeem the Indians, he thought, they must be reborn as farmers. But the Cayuse had not participated in the pilgrimage to St. Louis, and they wanted neither Christianity nor agriculture. Marcus grew despondent, and Narcissa's diaries chart her sadness. Her spirits glowed briefly with the birth of a daughter named Alice, but plunged when the toddler drowned two years later.

Slowly, Marcus decided the way to save the Indians was to immerse them in a large community of civilized people, and that meant attracting settlers. In 1842 he traveled to Boston, persuaded the Board to extend his mission, and returned in 1843 in a caravan. In the next few years a procession of wagons etched ruts in the mission road. A community grew, including several orphans adopted by Narcissa.

In a cruel turn, the settlers that Marcus had imagined as agents of Indian redemption instead carried measles to which Natives were not resistant. He could help the newcomers but not the Cayuse, half of whom perished in 1847. Watching their people die, some warriors discerned a plot to murder them and take their land. Their customs taught that a shaman whose patients died should be killed. Thus the elements of tragedy converged in late November 1847.

On November 29, two chiefs entered the mission kitchen. As one diverted Whitman's attention, the other killed the unsuspecting doctor with a tomahawk. Others murdered Narcissa outside the kitchen door, and twelve in all were killed. About forty-seven residents were captured, but a few escaped to spread the news. The mountain man Joe Meek, whose half-Indian daughter had lived under Narcissa's wing and died as a captive, galloped east to report the disaster in Washington, D.C. Shocked legislators responded in 1848 by creating Oregon Territory, a sprawling district to be policed by the Army, embracing today's Washington, Oregon, Idaho, and parts of Montana and Wyoming.

THE BLACK ROBES

Jesuit Father Pierre-Jean De Smet and Indian leaders, Fort Vancouver, 1859.

Native Americans called them "black robes"—Catholic fathers who brought the Roman faith to the New World. The first masses in the Pacific Northwest occurred on the ships of Spanish explorers. Yet it was the English, citizens of a mainly Protestant nation, who sponsored the first Catholic missions. Employees of England's Hudson's Bay Company were largely French-Canadian and *métis* (mixed French and Indian), and most were baptized Catholics. The company also hired Catholic Iroquois from the east, who told Northwest Natives about the black robes.

In 1834, Dr. John McLoughlin, head of the Hudson's Bay post at Fort Vancouver, asked company directors to dispatch priests to serve his Catholic flock. The request was fulfilled in 1838 when Franciscan Fathers François Blanchet and Modeste Demers arrived from eastern Canada. Demers founded St. Francis Xavier Mission at Cowlitz Farm under the slope of Mount Saint Helens, and Blanchet went to the Willamette Valley. There he devised a pictorial catechism, the Catholic Ladder—an illustrated timeline that displayed the events of sacred history for Native audiences. It was so popular as a primer that rival Protestants made their own version.

Meanwhile, Plateau Indians learned of the black robes from the Iroquois. Although Protestant missionaries were already active among them, the Plateau Indians sent two delegates to St. Louis in 1839, where they met Belgian-born Jesuit Pierre-Jean De Smet. Convinced of the Natives' desire to learn the faith, the energetic De Smet arrived on the Plateau in 1841 and began a network of missions that soon dotted the region. In 1842 he met Blanchet and Demers, and the trio coordinated their efforts. By 1848, twenty-eight Catholic citadels were in place, compared with fifteen for the Protestants. Neither denomination was wildly successful in winning or retaining converts, but Catholics were more effective. Natives evidently found Catholicism's colorful liturgy and vestments more enticing than Protestant austerity. The politically adroit De Smet was respected wherever he traveled, and Catholics were more willing to work on the Indians' own spiritual terms, tolerating a blend of Christian principle and aboriginal belief.

Tensions inevitably arose between Catholics and Protestants who, after all, had a history of holy wars dating to Luther's day. Protestants thought Catholic fathers were agents of the Hudson's Bay Company, secret promoters of British claims to Oregon country. They envied the Catholics' success in winning converts, and charged them with pandering to heathenism. The black robes, for their part, embellished their Catholic Ladders with images of Protestants plunging to the maw of hell. After Presbyterians Marcus and Narcissa Whitman were killed by Cayuse tribesmen in 1847, Whitman's colleague, the Rev. Henry Spalding, accused Catholics of inciting the murders. In truth, a Catholic priest was first on the scene after the atrocity and gave the Whitmans a Christian burial.

Hard feelings deepened after Washington Territory was created in 1853, and growing numbers of immigrants blamed Indian resistance on Catholic intrigue. When Yakima people under Chief Kamiakin defied resettlement to reservations and killed trespassing white miners in 1855, Army troops torched the Catholic Sainte Croix Mission on Ahtanum Creek (now Saint Joseph's Mission, near Yakima), on the mistaken premise that the killings were encouraged by priests.

Despite the adversity, Catholic missions continued to spread. Like their sectarian rivals, the Protestants, Catholic priests were as important as explorers and fur traders in raising outside awareness of the region that became Washington.

The Oregon Trail, engraving of 1869.

PIONEER SETTLEMENT

IMPERIAL TUG-OF-WAR

What? You Young Yankee-Noodle, Strike Your Own Father!
Punch *cartoon, 1846.*

When Spain's Bruno de Heceta landed on Washington's coast in 1775, claiming it for his country, he scarcely dreamed it would be a point of conflict for seven decades. As explorers learned more of the Northwest, it emerged as part of what cartographers called Oregon—after an Origan River once thought to exist there. It was vaguely bounded by Russian Alaska on the north, the Rockies to the east, and Spanish California in the south. Spain was ousted by Britain's naval might, and overextended Russia could not push its control south. England's claims sprang from voyages by Drake, Cook, and Vancouver, expeditions by Alexander MacKenzie, Simon Fraser, and David Thompson, and the commerce of its fur traders. Yet Britain was challenged by upstart America. Spain transferred its claims to the U.S. by an 1819 treaty—as far north as latitude 54° 40', the fringe of Russian Alaska.

England's navy ruled the seas, but she doubted the wisdom of establishing direct control over Oregon. Thus, she signed a pact with the U.S. in 1818, creating joint occupancy of the region. But in truth, England was in the driver's seat, for London's Hudson's Bay Company monopolized the fur trade. Yankee visitors were few and far between. Yet America's statesmen from Jefferson onward spun a national vision that stretched from sea to sea: a "manifest destiny."

Diplomats managed to negotiate a Canadian–U.S. boundary along the 49th parallel—at least from the Great Lakes to the Rockies—yet the Northwest frontier remained ill-defined. By 1840 three options seemed possible: America's northern border might coincide with Spain's claim of 54° 40'. It might, alternatively, follow latitude 49° to the Pacific. Or (as Britain hoped) it might track the 49th parallel to the Rockies, then follow the Columbia in a southwest arc to the sea. Had England won, the lion's share of Washington would be in Canada.

England's prospects seemed secure, but the winds shifted in the 1840s when American settlers, lured by dreams of lush farms, followed the Oregon Trail. The orations of U.S. congressmen assumed a swelling bluster, stoked by missionary labors. In 1844, Democratic presidential candidate James K. Polk won on the platform "Fifty-four forty or fight!" It seemed England and America might clash over Oregon. Yet Polk's margin of victory was razor thin, and the feisty slogan was just a rallying cry. More interested in fighting Mexico for California, he betrayed the Oregon war hawks in his own party. Months after taking office he proposed accepting the 49th parallel, to run straight through Vancouver Island—a scheme that would have placed Victoria in the United States.

The Hudson's Bay Company fought the compromise, which meant losing not only Victoria but Fort Vancouver on the lower Columbia, its artery for furs. But the fur trade was now in decline, and Britain's leaders were loath to risk war over the company's fading prospects. In the Oregon Treaty of 1846, England agreed to latitude 49° as the boundary, with the proviso that Victoria and Vancouver Island remain in British Canada.

From the Oregon Trail to Elliott Bay

Seattle, about 1860, with the house of mill owner Henry Yesler (foreground).

The mingled urges of religion, opportunity, and enterprise jostled in people's heads in the 1830s, inspiring folks who were willing to risk a move. "Whoo ha! Go it boys! We're in a perfect *Oregon fever*," declared an 1845 newspaper in Independence, Missouri, staging point for the Oregon Trail's covered wagon caravans.

By then the rush was under way. The first convoy left Missouri in 1841 and, in the "Great Migration" of 1843, nearly 900 people joined the exodus. By mid-century, 12,000 Americans called the Oregon country home. By the 1880s, when railroads replaced wagons, nearly 400,000 pilgrims had braved the 2,000-mile trail. At first, most settled in the Willamette Valley, but in 1846 England and America signed a treaty giving lands north of the Columbia to the U.S., all the way to the 49th parallel. Then the migration spilled north, toward Puget Sound.

The first American settlement there was Tumwater (first called New Market), in 1845. Colonization was spurred by the 1850 Donation Claims Act, giving 320 acres to anyone who settled before December and stayed for four years—and twice as much acreage to married couples. That was followed by a law giving 160 acres to individuals and 320 to couples who came by 1855. Among the first takers was Colonel Isaac Ebey, who scouted the Sound in 1850, eventually settling on a lovely Whidbey Island prairie above Admiralty Inlet—today Ebey's Landing National Historical Preserve. On his way, Ebey passed Elliott Bay. His letters praising the harbor and its Duwamish Valley as "rich bottom land" lured other settlers northward.

First was the seven-member Luther Collins party, which homesteaded near present-day Boeing Field in September 1851. Best remembered is the Arthur Denny clan from Illinois, twenty-two strong, who arrived at Alki Point (in present-day West Seattle) on November 13, 1851. The following February, seeking deeper water to ease shipment of the logs they were selling to San Francisco, they claimed Elliott Bay's east shore. They were soon joined by physician-storekeeper "Doc" Maynard and by Henry Yesler, who built a steam-driven sawmill, backbone of the hamlet's pioneer economy.

Yet the land they took wasn't vacant. Seventeen Duwamish villages were strewn along the bay, the river, and what Ebey had called Lake Geneva—today's Lake Washington. Led by a man named Sealth, or Seattle, they welcomed the newcomers for the blankets and tools they brought. Immigrants were also security against raids by marauding Canadian tribes, such as a daring 1856 attack on Steilacoom when 100 northerners stole the entire potato harvest. (The looters were chased by American sailors, who cornered them on Hood Canal and killed twenty-seven, including a chief.) It was Seattle, in fact, who invited Maynard to open his Elliott Bay store, and Maynard who suggested adopting the chief's name as the village's own. There were some tense times between Natives and colonizers, but under Seattle, the Duwamish remained peaceful.

Farther north, Colonel Ebey was not so lucky. Veterans of the band that attacked Steilacoom came back in 1857, set on revenge. Their customs taught that a chief's death in war demanded an enemy leader's head in return. Ebey, they discovered, was such a leader. On August 11 they beached their canoes below the bluffs at Ebey's Landing, spoke with the colonel to confirm his identity, and left. That night the warriors returned, shot him, and severed his head for a trophy.

The Birth of Washington Territory

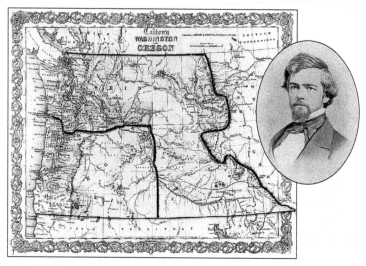

LEFT: Map of Washington Territory at its greatest extent, 1859–63.
RIGHT: Isaac Stevens, Washington's first territorial governor.

Covered wagons brought waves of newcomers who settled on Native lands and brought illnesses that laid waste to Indian villages. Ravaged by disease, many Indians were too demoralized to fight back, but some did. When Cayuse warriors killed missionaries Marcus and Narcissa Whitman near present-day Walla Walla, Washington, in 1847, a panic put Oregon country on the fast track to American union. Seeking army protection, settlers petitioned Congress for territorial status. Lawmakers agreed, and Oregon became a U.S. Territory in 1848. In its first guise, Oregon Territory included far more than what we know today as Oregon. It embraced the whole Northwest, including today's Oregon, Washington, and Idaho, as well as the parts of Montana and Wyoming west of the continental divide.

Pioneers trickled north to Puget Sound as early as 1845, and Seattle was born in 1852. There were 4,000 people on the Sound in 1853. From the start they grumbled that politicians far to the south on the Willamette controlled territorial purse strings. On November

25, 1852, some of them met at Monticello (present-day Longview, Washington) to ask Congress for a new territory north of the Columbia River, to be called Columbia. Even most Willamette men agreed that Oregon Territory was too big to be governed, so the north's secession was painless. Joseph Lane, Oregon's delegate to Congress, recommended the separation himself, and the only dispute concerned the new region's name. A Kentucky senator thought George Washington should be honored by the name of a territory. A few protested that another Washington—besides the nation's capital—would cause confusion, but Lane was happy to drop the Columbia name to grease the legislative process.

A bill creating Washington Territory passed with flying colors and was signed by President Fillmore on March 2, 1853. The new Washington was hardly less cumbersome than the original Oregon. From 1853 to 1859, it comprised today's Evergreen State, plus northern Idaho and western Montana. When Oregon attained statehood in 1859, today's southern Idaho and part of western Wyoming were added to Washington. Only in 1863, with the creation of Idaho Territory, did it assume today's dimensions.

The Washington Territory's easy birth was welcomed, but its first decade was a cradle of conflict and comic opera. Its first governor was Isaac Stevens, an empire builder who imagined Puget Sound as the navel of trade between New York and Asia—once a railway umbilical was built. But Stevens was headstrong and thin-skinned. When Indian wars erupted over his high-speed scheme to shunt Natives to reservations, farms were threatened and Stevens accused families of mixed Indian and European descent (the *métis*) of aiding the Indians. He proclaimed martial law and ordered settlers into blockhouses, actions that many opposed.

When Stevens prepared to try five resisters in military court, the territory's chief justice, Edward Lander, ordered Stevens arrested for contempt. The governor returned the favor by jailing the judge. When Lander retaliated by fining Stevens, the governor pardoned himself. Things sorted themselves out, but only after Stevens departed for Washington, D.C., in 1857, as Washington Territory's delegate to Congress. His life climaxed with characteristic bravura in 1862, when he died as a Union Army general, leading a charge at the Second Battle of Bull Run.

Henry Smith, Governor Stevens, and Chief Seattle

Chief Seattle and Henry Smith.

In 1887 the *Seattle Sunday Star* ran a story by Dr. Henry A. Smith, in which the aging physician recalled a meeting of Isaac Stevens, Washington Territory's first governor, and the Indian elder called Seattle. They met at a waterfront gathering—exactly when, Smith didn't say—where Stevens announced a plan to move Natives to reservations. Smith's memory of the chief's reply was gilded in his own Victorian prose. Aside from his recall, there was no record that Seattle had given the speech. Yet Smith's reminiscence became part of local lore and in the 1960s, through history's whims, it won fame as a manifesto of ecological values and aboriginal rights. In one version, embellished for modern tastes, it inaugurated the first Earth Day in 1970.

Chief Seattle, according to Smith, was resigned to accepting reservations. Yet, placing a hand on the governor's head and raising the other to the sky, the imposing chief foretold the haunting of future generations by the spirits of the displaced. He prophesied that "when the last red man shall have perished from the earth and his memory among white men shall have become a myth, these shores will swarm with the invisible dead of my tribe." Deliberately or not, Smith made the chief seem noble, the governor puny.

Stevens was indeed physically small, but he had a huge will. First in his West Point class of 1839, he rose to major general in the Mexican War and groomed himself for politics. In 1853 he became governor of newly minted Washington Territory. His first task was to make peace between Indians and the immigrants who took Native lands under the Donation Claims Act. As elsewhere, America's policy was to sign treaties with Indian leaders, transferring land title to the government. Homesteaders could then settle, while Natives were moved to reserves as government wards, to be slowly trained in modern ways.

Eager to prove his mettle, Stevens arranged councils with Indian leaders around the territory. Stevens coaxed some chiefs to forsake ancestral lands for reserves, but conceded their right to fish in traditional sites—a weighty compromise, as time would show. Not all Native leaders attended the meetings, though, and some who did had second thoughts—especially when miners trespassed on reserves. The upshot was the "Yakima War" between strongly resistant Indians, settler militias, and the army. Scores were killed, but fighting ended in 1858, when troops under Colonel George Wright routed a Native confederacy near present-day Spokane. At what is now known as Horse Slaughter Camp they killed 700 Indian ponies, leaving the bones to bleach as proof of the army's might. Wright arrested Qualchin, a Yakima warrior he blamed for killing six miners. In his terse report, he wrote: "Qual-chian came to me at 9 o'clock this morning and at 9-1/4 a.m. he was hung." After hanging several others, he declared "The war is closed."

Stevens's plan to ease tensions between Natives and newcomers had produced the opposite. Reservations didn't solve the Indians' plight, and issues of resource use still haunt relations between Indians and non-Natives. We can't be sure if Chief Seattle was the soothsayer Smith remembered, or that he gave the oration Smith recalled. The waterfront meeting may never have happened, though Smith wasn't known as a liar. The chief was a friend of early settlers—on that there is plenty of evidence. Still, the words Smith put in Seattle's mouth sound like the voice of conscience, and they ring of essential—if not literal—truth.

BLACK PIONEERS

Descendants of George Washington Bush at the Bush Prairie homestead near Tumwater.

Among the pilgrims who braved the Oregon Trail, a few belonged to racial minorities. In 1850, 207 "free colored" people lived in Oregon Territory. There might have been more, but most pioneers did not extend a welcome. The quandary of slavery lay thick in the air, and settlers were split-minded on the question. A form of slavery existed among Northwest Indians, and had from time immemorial. A few newcomers brought black slaves with them. Some, like Oregon's first territorial governor Joseph Lane, thought Northwest soil would support plantations worked by slave labor. Others differed, and in 1843 a gathering in the Willamette Valley voted to outlaw slavery. But they didn't want black settlers, either, for in 1844 they ordered Negroes—free or slave—to leave within three years. Those who refused would be flogged at six-month intervals.

The law was probably never enforced, but it convinced George Washington Bush, one of Puget Sound's first colonists, to bypass the Willamette and head north of the Columbia. Bush's origins are obscure. His contemporaries considered him "colored" (and he concurred), though it is unclear if he was African-American. Born in Philadelphia around 1790, his mother was an Irish maid and his dark-skinned father may have come from India. Whatever his lineage, he was deemed a "free mulatto." Against the odds, he became a prosperous cattle trader in Missouri, where he married a white wife and had several sons. With Michael T. Simmons, he led a group of 31 Americans—some of whom he bankrolled—over the Oregon Trail in 1844. Along the way he told a companion that "he should watch, when we got to Oregon, what usage was awarded to people of color, and if he could not have a free man's rights he would seek the protection of the Mexican Government in California or New Mexico."

Oregon's black exclusion resolution had just been passed, but instead of heading south, the Bush-Simmons party turned north to Puget Sound. Near the Hudson's Bay Company post at Fort Nisqually, Simmons founded New Market in November 1845, soon renamed Tumwater. Bush started a farm nearby, on what became Bush's Prairie. The tiny fellowship survived on help from Fort Nisqually and local Indians. By the 1850s it was attracting new settlers (including Nathaniel Crosby of Maine, grandfather of singer Bing Crosby, born in Tacoma in 1901). Bush, a seasoned businessman, was among the community's leaders.

Still, Bush had a legal problem. Federal laws did not permit Negroes or mulattos to make land claims, so he had no title to the earth he cultivated. In 1854, friends in Washington's new territorial legislature petitioned Congress to grant him an exemption. In 1855 the request was approved. But while his neighbors valued Bush's economic contributions, they weren't ready to embrace him as a political equal, for the territorial assembly denied him voting rights.

Despite Bush's example, early Washington was not a magnet for black settlers. By 1900 there were only 2,500 black residents in the Evergreen State. Bush nevertheless helped pave the way for some other successful black pioneers, such as hotelkeeper William Grose and publisher Horace Cayton of Seattle, as well as "Black George" Washington, the Virginia-born son of an African-American slave who founded Centerville (Centralia) in 1872. George Washington Bush died in April 1863, shortly after President Lincoln issued his Emancipation Proclamation. Had he survived to be 100, he would doubtless have relished witnessing Washington's statehood in 1889, and seeing his son, William O. Bush, elected to a two-year term in the first state legislature.

Looking over Cowlitz Glacier from the Cowlitz Rocks, Mount Rainier.

FROM BIG TREES TO BIG SKY: THE EARLY DAYS OF WASHINGTON TERRITORY

THE PIG WAR

Third Artillery soldiers in dress uniforms, American Camp, San Juan Island, October 1859.

On June 15, 1859, an American named Lyman Cutlar spied a pig rooting in his garden on San Juan Island. The Berkshire boar belonged to Charles Griffen, head of the Hudson's Bay Company's Belle Vue Farm. Griffen and his superior, James Douglas—governor of Britain's Vancouver Island—were confident that the San Juan Islands belonged to England, and they considered the Americans squatters. The pig had visited Cutlar's garden before, and this time he shot it. He offered to make good the loss, but Griffen demanded $100—a staggering sum for the day, which Cutlar refused to pay. When Douglas threatened to arrest Cutlar, the escalating conflict brought England and America to the verge of war.

The boar's death magnified a devilishly ambiguous detail in the Oregon Treaty, the 1846 pact that established the boundary between Canada and the United States. The treaty said the border should follow the 49th parallel "to the middle of the channel which separates the continent from Vancouver's Island; and thence southerly through the middle of the said channel, and of Fuca's straits to the Pacific Ocean." But the statesmen who signed it didn't know there were two main channels through the islands: westerly Haro Strait, and Rosario Strait to the east. If Haro was the frontier, San Juan and its sister islands lay in the United States. If Rosario was the boundary, most belonged to Canada.

When Douglas threatened Cutlar, American settlers appealed to the U.S. Army for protection. Without requesting higher approval, General William S. Harney, commander of American forces in Washington Territory, ordered Captain George E. Pickett and sixty-six infantrymen from Fort Bellingham to the island. Pickett pitched camp near Cutlar's cabin, and Lt. Henry Robert of the Army Engineers oversaw construction of an earthen redoubt with fourteen cannons. Meanwhile, Douglas ordered British warships to the site with orders to force Pickett to withdraw. But Pickett wouldn't back down, even though by August, American troops (increased to 461) confronted five British ships carrying over 2,000 sailors.

Nothing was initially known of the crisis in London and Washington, D.C. For a few weeks, the tinderbox might have exploded. In August, however, Britain's Rear Admiral R. Lambert Baynes arrived. Sizing things up, he declared the Royal Navy would not risk war "over a squabble about a pig." U.S. President James Buchanan learned of the situation as well. "It would be a shocking event," he said, "if . . . two nations should be precipitated into a war respecting the possession of a small island."

In September, Buchanan dispatched Winfield Scott, Army commander-in-chief, to Puget Sound. Scott persuaded Douglas that the island should be jointly occupied by American and British garrisons until common sense resolved the dispute. Pickett's men were replaced by a small U.S. force at American Camp and Harney was transferred. In 1860, Britain established English Camp with its picturesque blockhouse—still standing—south of present-day Roche Harbor. Far from fighting, over the next twelve years the servicemen socialized and celebrated holidays together. Along the way America fought its Civil War. In 1863 Confederate Major General George E. Pickett, cursed again by ill-advised orders (those of Robert E. Lee), led his disastrous charge at Gettysburg. Lieutenant Robert, who built Pickett's fortifications, won fame as author of *Robert's Rules of Order*.

In 1871, England and the United States submitted their dispute to Germany's Kaiser Wilhelm I for arbitration. On October 21, 1872, the Kaiser issued his verdict: Haro Strait was the boundary, and the San Juans were American. The Pig War's sole victim was Griffen's Berkshire boar.

THE MINING FRONTIER

Coal miners, Coal Creek, 1880s.

Washington Territory never had a bonanza on the scale of the 1848 California gold rush, but its creeks yielded some storied strikes. Moreover, mining was a blood-pumping catalyst for other beginnings: ranching, business, and gold in another guise—wheat.

Miners first hit pay dirt near Fort Colvile, northwest of present-day Spokane, in 1855. In seeking the wealth, some prospectors trespassed on Yakima Indian land, and six paid with their lives—one cause of Indian wars of the late 1850s. The Fraser River gold rush followed in 1858. Though centered in Canada, it lured stampeders to the falls of Whatcom Creek. A general store of stout brick was built on pilings above the mudflats of Bellingham Bay, designed to double as a vault for Fraser River gold. But Whatcom didn't become the San Francisco it aspired to be, for British authorities made Victoria the entry point to the Fraser goldfields. The throng that camped at Whatcom Creek vanished overnight.

More important were strikes in 1860 on Oro Fino Creek, east of present-day Lewiston, Idaho. In one frenzied year the backcountry on Nez Perce Indian land became Washington's population center. Discoveries billowed out to the Salmon River, Boise Basin, and Virginia City in today's Montana, where tent cities ("rag towns") burgeoned, filled by men with gold addiction's manic gaze.

The stampeders' numbers swelled briefly to 75,000. Washington's gold had a national impact, priming the Union's economy and helping finance victory in the Civil War. The creek beds were ravished by placer mining, however, commencing a history of salmon habitat destruction.

The rush caused a boom of steamboat traffic up the Columbia and Snake. It changed Walla Walla, site of an Army post, into the supply hub north of Mormon Utah. Walla Walla became—briefly—Washington's biggest town and rival to Olympia as territorial capital. In the Civil War era, Olympia lawmakers were mainly supporters of Abraham Lincoln, while the new miners were often southern sympathizers. Sensing that growing numbers of eastern miners might elect Democrats and force movement of the capital to Walla Walla, Olympia Republicans converted to the idea of territorial status for Idaho—approved by Congress in 1863. Thus Washington assumed its present configuration on the map, and Walla Walla lost its political clout.

In the long run it wasn't gold but a humble treasure—coal—that added most to Washington mining's bottom line. San Francisco's growth required coal for heating and energy, and the coming of railroads in the 1880s multiplied the demand. Thick coal seams marbled the Cascade Mountains and the banks of Puget Sound. In 1853, a Bellingham Bay mine shipped 150 tons to San Francisco, and thereafter many settlements got their boost as gritty coal towns. By 1900, Seattle was the coast's major coaling port.

Before World War I, miners worked ten- or twelve-hour days at twenty cents an hour, and coal mining brought the first sizable influx of African-Americans in the 1880s, often as strikebreakers. In that decade, the territory's black population grew from 180 to more than 1600. Some hamlets adapted over time to become gleaming cities of glass and steel. Greater Bellevue, for example, began partly in the 1860s as the neighbor towns of Coal Creek and Newcastle, the latter named for the English coal town. A total of 150 million tons of black earth were dug there over the next century. Other communities like Roslyn, east of Snoqualmie Pass, became rust-roofed derelicts when oil and electricity began to replace coal in the 1920s, and strikes hamstrung production. Like the gold booms, coal fever produced its share of ghost towns.

The Steamboat Era

Stern-wheel steamboat on the Columbia River, 1915.

People at Fort Vancouver beheld an omen of the future on April 10, 1836. It was the arrival of the Beaver, the first steamboat on the Pacific Coast. Built near London for the Hudson's Bay Company in 1835, the chunky 101-foot vessel labored around Cape Horn under sail. Her paddle wheels were mounted on her port and starboard sides at the fort.

Before railroads, water was the best highway and Washington boasted two great waterways—the Columbia-Snake River system and Puget Sound. The trend heralded by the *Beaver* blossomed in the 1850s. For fifty years, steamboats reigned where there was water and people wanted to go. Woodcutters scoured riverbanks to feed the vessels' hunger for fuel. Flat-bottomed stern-wheelers were introduced, their boilers mounted on the foredeck, boosting their power to plough into winds and currents and reducing their draft to a foot of water. The Northwest's torrents, tumbling through canyons and coulees, presented special challenges. On the Columbia there were three fearsome cataracts: the Cascades, the Grand Dalles, and Celilo Falls. Before dams made today's Columbia and Snake into a chain of slack-water lakes, these stretches had to be portaged. Boats carried freight to the rapids' brink, offloaded cargo for carriage to the other side, then all was loaded on another vessel.

Stern-wheel travel gained its full head of steam in the 1860s, when gold strikes in eastern Washington Territory created a stampede market. Most profits went to John C. Ainsworth's Oregon Steam Navigation Company. Ainsworth gained a monopoly over traffic to the interior. He built rail lines around the cataracts, and in 1861 he sent two daring pilots—Ephraim Baughman and Leonard White— up the Snake in the 125-foot *Colonel Wright* to see how near they could get to the Oro Fino goldfields. They churned their way as far as the Clearwater River's Big Eddy, forty-five miles below the mines, paving the way for an influx of wealth seekers. The demand for tools and whisky was so steep that Ainsworth charged ten times the shipping rates on the Missouri.

The stampede was over by 1870, but the boom continued as wheat replaced gold in steamer holds. Wheat cultivation began around Walla Walla and spread north to the Palouse Hills, pierced by the Snake's chasms. Shippers devised ingenious ways to get the grain, hauled to canyon rims, to landings sometimes 2,000 feet below. One method shot grain to the bottom in four-inch pipes, where it was sacked and loaded. Gravity-driven trams were also used—similar to ski lifts. Fruit was another cargo, as farmers planted orchards on the Snake's benchlands in the 1870s.

On occasion people died when boilers blew and vessels sank. One of the worst mishaps occurred aboard the *Annie Faxon* in 1893, when an explosion killed eight. Still, sternwheelers knit the land together, and their whistles, belching stacks, and churning wheels seized the fancy of plateau settlers. When railroads came in the 1880s the paddle-wheel era entered its decline. By 1918, it was over. Yet the construction of locks in the 1960s and 1970s injected new vigor into the rivers as commercial arteries, worked by barges and diesel tugs. Paddle wheelers even made a comeback in tourism—now diesel-powered, to be sure. In a commemorative gesture, the first boat to pass through all four of the Snake's new locks in 1975 was the stern-wheeler *Portland*—a distant echo of the *Colonel Wright*'s trailblazing journey of 1861.

CHINESE PIONEERS

Early Seattle merchant Chin Chun Hock (with cane) and business partners.

Among the throngs lured to Washington's mining frontier were many Chinese. Chinese laborers began coming to America in the 1840s. They took part in California's gold rush and worked on farms and later on railroad gangs. News of Washington's Oro Fino gold strike in 1860 brought hundreds of Chinese north, and others followed when smaller strikes occurred on the Columbia. Single men, they toiled under contract for Chinese firms based in San Francisco or Portland. The 1868 Burlingame Treaty permitted Chinese to freely enter America, and Chinese mining companies established big work camps along the Columbia.

Washington's gold rush was over by 1870, yet the Chinese scoured diggings abandoned by others, discovering much overlooked gold. When railroads, coal mining, logging, and fish canning energized Washington's economy in the 1870s and 1880s, labor contractors like Seattle's Chin Hock and Chin Gee Hee supplied Chinese hands for those jobs. They were not welcomed by other workers, who viewed them as rivals and strikebreakers—"Heathen Johns" who drove down wages and worked on the Sabbath.

Such views prompted the nationwide Chinese Exclusion Act in 1882, halting Chinese immigration for ten years. The law also prevented resident Chinese from becoming citizens. Children born in America to Chinese parents were citizens, but they still suffered discrimination—and not many were born, since so few Chinese women immigrated. The ban was renewed in 1894 and extended indefinitely in 1904. That meant that Chinatowns became enclaves of aging single men, governed by fraternal associations, secret societies, and gangs. (The exclusion act was lifted in 1943 because China was an ally in the war against Japan.) On occasion, anti-Chinese riots erupted. In November 1885, a mob evicted Tacoma's entire Chinese community, about 700 people. The city's Chinatown was burned, and four to six people died. In an echo of that atrocity, most of Seattle's Chinese were expelled in February 1886. Yet some Chinese labor still flowed into the area illegally.

Despite adversity, Chinese pioneers helped shape Washington's identity. Chinese were the most numerous of the region's early Asian settlers, and—despite the long immigration ban—people of Chinese heritage still represent Washington's third-largest Asian community, after Japanese- and Filipino-Americans. Two-thirds of the labor force that built the Northern Pacific Railroad was Chinese. Chinese labor was so vital to the early canneries that owners thought the industry would collapse without them.

Enforcement of exclusion statutes was not airtight, and bigotry was not insurmountable, as shown by one family's history. Lung Sing Luke came from south China to work in the United States in the early 1900s, then returned to Kwangtung Province, where he married and fathered a son in 1925. Leaving his family in Asia, he returned to Seattle and eventually persuaded authorities to permit his wife and infant son to join him. His son excelled in school, fought in World War II, and gained citizenship after the exclusion law's repeal. After earning a law degree at the University of Washington, Wing Luke of Kwangtung Province became Washington's assistant attorney general, serving for five years, and was elected to Seattle's city council in 1960. It was a breakthrough, and by 1989—the centennial of Washington statehood—more elective posts were held by Chinese-Americans in Seattle and King County than anywhere in the country. In 1997 Gary Locke became Washington's governor—the first Asian-American to occupy a state house.

The Mosquito Fleet

Seattle's Coleman dock, hub of the Mosquito Fleet, 1915.

In early times, Puget Sound was Washington's marine highway, and steamboats were its lifeline. Among Puget Sounders, nothing evokes more nostalgia than the "mosquito fleet"—the throng of privately run steamboats that once linked towns on the 2,000-mile shore of Washington's inland sea. Sidewheelers, sternwheelers, and propeller-driven, some 2,500 of these vessels plied the Sound between the 1850s and the Great Depression.

The first steamers—the *Beaver* and the *Otter*—were owned by the Hudson's Bay Company. Puget Sound was raw and remote, however, and early pioneers didn't often see the Hudson's Bay boats. The first Seattleites hired Indian canoes as water taxis. That changed in 1853 when the Sound got its first American-built mail boat, the *Fairy*, a sixty-five-foot sidewheeler that arrived from San Francisco. But the petite *Fairy* churned a modest wake. Distressingly slow, she was so unstable that, rounding Alki Point, she rolled on her side with one wheel above water. She was soon confined to the straighter Olympia-to-Steilacoom route. Her wings stopped when her boiler blew and she sank to the bottom.

Before 1871 navigation was unregulated, so many boats were jerry-built. By the 1880s, however, the fleet was reliable, and in 1900 there were forty-eight shipping companies in Seattle alone. Bewhiskered and clad in nautical caps and blue serge, the best flotilla captains cut an impressive appearance and enjoyed high esteem. Fog and tricky tides challenged the captains' skills, and early navigation was more art than science. Veteran pilots negotiated foul weather by "dog and whistle navigation." A blast of the whistle was sent reverberating off bluffs and headlands, setting dogs to barking—and captains reckoned the distance to shore by earshot. It usually worked, but disasters happened. The worst occurred in January 1904, when the *Clallam* sank near Port Townsend, killing fifty-four passengers.

To make steam, the vessels burned acres of wood—as much as six to eight cords a day. Passengers were sometimes segregated by gender, with ladies riding aft where they crocheted and tended children, and men sitting forward in spittoon-garnished smoking salons. Most famous of the early boats was the 140-foot sidewheeler *Eliza Anderson*, brought to the Sound in 1859. "Old Anderson" made a slow-and-steady nine knots and earned handsome profits hauling every sort of cargo, from mail to livestock to pianos. She acquired a carnival flair when her owners fitted a calliope to her boilers, to delight crowds with patriotic tunes as she steamed into port. Yet beneath her charm she was a savage competitor. She was suspected of smuggling Chinese workers, and she rammed one of her rivals—the *George E. Starr*—off Whidbey Island in the 1880s. In her last escapade, she ferried stampeders to Alaska during the gold rush, but ran aground and ended as firewood.

Steamer races enlivened waterfront towns. Champion of the fleet was the *Tacoma*, which averaged twenty knots on runs between 1913 and 1930—the world's speediest single-screw commercial steamer. But interurban railways and then Henry Ford doomed the fleet after World War I. Vessels were sold for scrap or left to rot on beaches. The only steam-powered survivor of the jaunty armada is the 125-foot *Virginia V*, which barely escaped the scrap yard in World War II. The excursion trade kept her precariously afloat in the 1950s and '60s, as people slowly grew to value heritage and historical preservation. In 1973 she was put on the National Register of Historic Sites. Owned by the nonprofit *Virginia V* Foundation, restoration of her 1898 engine and pilothouse was completed in June 2002.

THE IRON HORSE
AND THE VISION OF
ECONOMIC EMPIRE

The Northern Pacific Railroad survey near the Green River.

5786-B

Empire Builders

Railroad tycoon James J. Hill

"Give us a railroad!" implored the Walla Walla *Watchman* in 1880. "Though it be a rawhide one with open passenger cars and a sheet iron boiler; anything on wheels drawn by an iron horse! But give us a railroad."

Railroading in Washington was in its infant stage when the *Watchman* pronounced its words. The Northwest's first lines were adjuncts to steamboats: mule-drawn trams built to bypass rough water on the Columbia. In 1875 the wheat country's first steam line was completed, a thirty-two-mile track connecting Walla Walla to the Columbia at Wallula. Built by physician Dorsey Baker, it featured wooden rails covered by strap iron. Despite its rough-hewn technology, the line made Baker rich. But bolder schemes were afoot, and visionaries already had realized their dream of a rail line linking the Atlantic and Pacific. The golden spike linking San Francisco to the East Coast was driven in 1869.

Events unfolded slower in the Northwest. Jay Cooke, aided by government rights-of-way and land-grant subsidies, began the Northern Pacific Railroad in 1870 at Duluth, Minnesota, while a western crew built a track from Kalama on the Columbia to a hamlet called Tacoma. Crews had orders to work toward one another, but Cooke went bankrupt in 1873 and the project languished. In 1881 Henry Villard won control of the company and, with financial wizardry, pushed the job through by 1883. A ribbon of steel finally linked Chicago and Tacoma, and a trip that took five months was slashed to five days.

Seattle seethed over upstart Tacoma's choice as the Northern Pacific's terminus and clamored for its own umbilical to the East. Its plea was heard by James J. Hill, an even greater empire builder than Villard. Hill began what became the Great Northern Railroad in St. Paul, Minnesota, in 1878. Without government land grants, he worked westward, relying on his skill as a land promoter to people the country served by feeder lines he built. "Give me enough Swedes and whisky," he boasted, "and I'll build a railroad to Hell!" The fact that he routed his tracks through Spokane, also served by the Northern Pacific, made that city the hub of what its boosters called the Inland Empire. By 1893 Hill's Great Northern road reached Seattle. The timing was right, for three years later gold was discovered in the Yukon. With its new link to eastern cities, Seattle grasped its breakthrough role as nerve center of the Klondike Stampede. When the city celebrated its coming-of-age at the Alaska-Yukon-Pacific Exposition in 1909, Hill gave the opening oration. That same year a third line was completed—the Chicago, Milwaukee, and St. Paul, or Milwaukee Road.

With the iron steed to haul crops and timber to distant markets, Washington embarked on a fast track toward national prominence. Towns sprouted at strategic points and received railroad christenings. Pullman was named for a sleeping-car tycoon. People in Pasco or Othello could order from the wish-books of Sears Roebuck or Montgomery Ward, acquiring an imagined sense of community with far-flung worlds. Rail links to ocean steamers enhanced the state's Far Eastern trade. But what liberated could also shackle. Farmers expected low freight rates when rails arrived to compete with steamboats. The river monopoly was overturned, but railroads then charged the most that markets would bear. The town of Yakima had to pull up stakes and move four miles, just to be where the railroad located its station.

GREAT EXPECTATIONS

Breaking virgin soil, Washington (postcard).

In the 1840s the Oregon Trail mystique spawned fancies of the Northwest as a land of milk and honey. Yet many easterners, if they thought of the region at all, imagined it as dank or desolate. Washington had an image problem, and in the late 1800s missionaries gave way to railroad barons and scenic postcards as evangelists of its promised land.

Railway promoters faced a daunting quandary in the 1870s and 1880s. To make money, they needed people to grow and harvest commodities they could haul, yet the regions they proposed to serve were thinly populated and commercially undeveloped. The railroad patriarchs—Jay Cooke, Henry Villard, and James J. Hill—answered the challenge with history's first great advertising campaign, designed to ignite an exodus from the East and invent markets out of vacant soil and big sky. The crusade, combining the tactics of Moses and P. T. Barnum, centered on furnishing peoples' minds with alluring images and promising them cheap land. Railroads, their boosters claimed, conjured profit out of thin air. "Railroads give actual value to lands," wrote George Henry Atkinson in 1878. "Complete the road from the Columbia to the Missouri and this strip, eighty miles wide and two thousand long . . . will acquire real worth."

There was also the appeal to freedom and self-reliance on the frontier's cutting edge. "PUBLIC ATTENTION Is now largely directed to the VAST NEW REGIONS Opened for Settlement by the completion of the NORTHERN PACIFIC RAILROAD," trumpeted a company flyer in 1884. "THERE IS AMPLE ROOM in this Great Belt of Productive and Prosperous Country FOR MILLIONS OF SETTLERS To secure COMFORTABLE HOMES and become INDEPENDENT." The Northern Pacific's advertising branch mobilized colonists abroad as well as in America. In 1883 it employed hundreds of agents in Europe exhorting emigration at fairs and country markets. "The West is purely a railroad enterprise," bragged one official. "We started it in our publicity department."

That boast was slightly exaggerated. Settlement had plenty of help from eastern editors of the Horace Greeley school ("Go West, young man!"), chambers of commerce, and the humble postcard. Scenic postcards got their start in Europe with the rise of tourism in Germany's Rhineland and the Alps. American travelers posted them home, and their trademark salutation "*Gruss aus*" was easily converted to the English "Greetings from . . ." The postcard's golden age dovetailed with steam locomotion's triumphant era, Washington's statehood, and the Alaska–Yukon gold bonanza. Bearing the explicit or implied banner "Greetings from Washington," millions of rosy-toned images heralding the state's wonders were mailed around the nation, streaked with heavenly blue and couched in a magical soft focus that kindles nostalgic smiles today. Most were designed to stir feelings of God's country, to summon prayerful feelings of awe. Some were broadside jokes, depicting men harvesting potatoes as big as boulders or cabbages the size of wash baskets. At the new century's dawn, these penny fortunetellers prophesied the future, and it was sprinkled with dollar signs, prospects of freedom, and open-ended prosperity.

The inviting image was created, the rail lines were built, and people came. In 1860, Washington Territory's population was only 12,000—and it then included Idaho and parts of Montana and Wyoming. By 1880 it was trimmed to its present boundaries but its human numbers had grown to 75,000. In the next decade—aided by completion of the Northern Pacific in 1883—they swelled to 350,000. By 1910, in the state's greatest population burst to date, Washington's numbers increased threefold, to well over one million.

EVENTFUL 1889

Spokane Falls volunteer fire department comet hose team, 1885.

"Vigorous life and strife are to be seen everywhere. The spirit of progress is in the air," wrote John Muir in 1888, after visiting Puget Sound. Muir, sage of environmentalism, nonetheless extolled the "white heat of work" unleashed by railways. On Washington's east side, Spokane Falls (today's Spokane) mirrored Muir's exhilaration. The town had just been chartered in 1881, but the Northern Pacific arrived that same year, there was a gold rush in the Coeur d'Alene Mountains, and Dutch banks invested in real estate. By 1889 its population approached 20,000.

Amid the exuberance, the territory aspired to statehood. Washingtonians resented taxes without representation and the fact that their territorial governors often spent little time in the region. Their population, swelling to 350,000 in the 1880s, sufficed for statehood, yet politics got in the way. Since Republicans dominated the territorial assembly, Democrats fought admitting a state likely to send foes to Congress. But in 1888 the GOP captured both houses in the nation's capitol, and Republican Benjamin Harrison unseated Grover Cleveland as president. With Washington statehood now in the cards, the lame-duck Cleveland approved a constitutional assembly, to begin at Olympia July 4, 1889.

Lawmakers were upstaged by the great fires that engulfed Seattle and Spokane Falls. Seattle's blaze began around 3 p.m. on June 6, ignited by burning glue in a cabinet shop. The fire chief was out of town—at a fire prevention meeting!—and most people stood back and gaped at the blaze. It roared through the night, consuming thirty business blocks. No one died, but the town was momentarily rid of its colossal rat problem. Upon the cinders arose the brick and sandstone structures that still define Seattle's south end.

The Spokane Falls fire exploded two months later, on August 4, when a boarding house caught fire next to the Northern Pacific depot. When the blaze was detected, a nearby hydrant failed to function, and things got out of hand. Next morning the sun rose over thirty-two scorched blocks in the business district. Surrounding towns responded generously, donating tents, cured hams, and other aid. As in Seattle, calamity stiffened civic backbone. "It was a blessing in disguise," someone said, "and the city will rise again, stronger and better than ever." That indeed happened—the town was rechristened Spokane in 1891—but a whiff of scandal tainted its rebirth. It seems that many donated food and relief items were carted to cellars in the town's elite neighborhoods. Two councilmen and a policeman were indicted by a grand jury, but they never came to trial. People spoke of the "ham council" that shielded them from justice.

Between the fires, Olympia's lawmakers convened on July 4. They worked through the summer and submitted their frothy charter (seven times the length of the U.S. Constitution) in an October referendum, which also settled some contentious issues and elected the state's first officials. The upshot was easy ratification and a Republican landslide. The all-male voters rejected women's suffrage by two to one (though women got the state ballot in 1910), and defeated liquor prohibition by a similar margin. In the hottest issue, Olympia remained the capital, despite challenges by Ellensburg and North Yakima. The eventful year climaxed on November 11, when President Harrison signed Washington's admission to the union. The nation's forty-second state would have to pay its way, though. A telegram reporting the news arrived in Olympia collect, and governor-to-be Elisha P. Ferry had to pay sixty-one cents before he could read it.

FISHERIES AND CANNERIES

The salmon harvest in Washington waters, about 1905.

In the 1920s, according to regional humor, when you met a person from Bellingham you extended your hand in a fish-tail motion. The town was home to Pacific American Fisheries, reputedly the world's largest fish cannery, and lay near Canada's Fraser River, funnel for one of the great sockeye runs. In early times, locals claimed, salmon ran so thick in the streams that farmers pitchforked wagonloads for fertilizer and pig feed. Yet by the 1920s overfishing thrust Washington's salmon into decline, and cannery profits sprang partly from stations in Alaska. Technology changed, the Pacific American cannery closed in 1966, and by the 1990s the Fraser run was the region's last robust salmon fishery.

The tale of Washington's fisheries is one of profit, depletion, and many species, from 400-pound halibut landed off Cape Flattery to the Puget tidelands' acres of clams. Champion of all was the athletic salmon, symbol of the wild Northwest. Washington's waters churned with five species: chinook, sockeye, coho, pink, and chum, plus their cousin the steelhead trout. Born in freshwater streams, they migrated to sea for several years, then returned to their birthplaces to breed and die. Ten to sixteen million per year once swam the Columbia River, and two million continued up the Snake.

That changed with the advent of fish canning. Canning reached the Columbia when Hapgood and Hume launched the first operation there in 1866. By 1880 there were fifty-five canneries on the river, and Puget Sound's first was built at Mukilteo in 1876. The Columbia yielded forty-three million pounds of chinook in 1883, and forty-six million pounds of all species in 1911. Puget Sound eclipsed that. The 1901 catch in the San Juans was so big that canneries couldn't process the fish, and more were thrown away than packed.

Competition was at first no-holds-barred. Salmon seemed endless and free for the taking—by whatever means. Barriers steered them into ponds and traps, and revolving fish wheels scooped up mighty fistfuls. Scandinavian, Finn, and Croatian skippers piloted gill net and purse seine boats, often leased from the canneries. After 1900 they sported gas engines. While overfishing reduced the runs, spawning beds fell victim to silting produced by logging, mining, farming, and pulp mills. Then came the big dams, starting with Bonneville and Grand Coulee in the 1930s. Fish ladders were installed at most of them, but Grand Coulee was deemed too high for ladders, dealing salmon stocks above the dam—and the Native fishery at Kettle Falls—a killing blow.

Biologists wagered on hatcheries to replenish exhausted runs, but that story has been mixed. Most of Washington's salmon now come from hatcheries, but despite the large federal and state investment, populations are a fraction of old-time levels. Besides, hatchery fish are less robust than wild salmon that spawn in free-running streams. They interbreed with dwindling wild stocks, reducing survival ability. Water quality, too, is a problem. A cocktail of pollutants, including human drugs, enters the "Salish Sea" (a new, fashionable label for Puget Sound, Juan de Fuca and Georgia straits, and the San Juan Archipelago). Many wild stocks are extinct or on the endangered list. To save them, preservationists propose tearing down dams. Two small, outdated dams on the Olympic Peninsula's Elwha River were in fact removed between 2011 and 2014, and there are promising signs of the return of salmon to its headwaters. The notion of breaching larger, newer dams on big rivers like the Snake, however, is hotly controversial. One threat to wild Pacific salmon was addressed in 2018, when Washington banned new leases for non-native Atlantic salmon fish farms. As for the fishing industry—once second to logging as a state enterprise—a shrinking fraternity of skippers keeps commercial operations alive, aided by government subsidies, the Alaska fishery, and nettlesome treaties with Canada that divide the runs. Northwesterners still think of the muscular salmon as an essential part of the region's identity. The salmon will likely endure, as a commodity and a reminder of the wisdom of ecological awareness. But wild salmon that spawn in streams may not.

The Timber Harvest

Early loggers and skid road, about 1890.

"Fifteen million acres of forest unacquainted with the axe." Albert Beveridge had Cuba in mind when he turned this phrase in 1898, but it spoke volumes about feelings toward timber in the heyday of industry and enterprise. No region better fit the description "big timber" than Washington. Today, after generations of harvests, Washington's trees are not so huge, but one-half of the Evergreen State is still blanketed by fir, cedar, hemlock, spruce, pine, maple, and alder—more than twenty-one million acres in all.

Commercial lumbering began with the Hudson's Bay Company. The firm built the Northwest's first sawmill at Camas in 1827, five miles east of Fort Vancouver. Settlers who came via the Oregon Trail were mainly farmers who considered forest patriarchs obstacles to agriculture. Beyond supplying wood for fuel, plank roads, and cabins, wilderness was a nuisance to be cleared away. But San Francisco's rise created new outlets for timber. Puget Sound sawmills sprouted to meet the demand—Yesler's at Seattle, Henry Roeder's at Whatcom, others at Port Blakely, Port Ludlow, and Port Gamble. Woodsmen cut trees in a slash-and-burn spirit. Washington's trees were mammoth by Maine or Minnesota standards. Ancient Douglas fir soared in groves 300 feet high.

Trees were cut by axemen and sawyers on springboards fifteen feet above the ground, leaving the trunk butt to rot. Oxen pulled the logs over "skid roads" to tidewater, where they went to market aboard lumber schooners. In the 1880s oxen were replaced by steam donkeys—moveable, cable-rigged engines that allowed cutting on terrain where animals couldn't go. At the same time, operators threaded railroads into remote canyons. Logging camps aimed to get everything of worth, get it quickly, and move on to get more. In 1880, 160 million board feet of timber were harvested. By 1890, it was over a billion. High-lead logging, which moved logs by cable systems strung from spar trees, began around 1910. Hills and valleys were denuded and soil washed downstream. The work was wasteful, low paying, and risky, yet the woods seemed endless.

The arrival of railways in the 1880s opened up Midwest markets, and created a demand for ties and trestles. More important was immigration to the Northwest, requiring wood for construction. With added demand caused by the damage from the 1906 San Francisco earthquake, Washington became the "sawdust empire"— the nation's leading timber producer, slipping behind Oregon only in 1938. Thanks to federal land-grant subsidies, millions of acres fell under railroad ownership. In 1900 James J. Hill, the railway magnate, sold 900,000 acres to his St. Paul friend Frederick Weyerhaeuser at $6 per acre, and guaranteed low freight rates on his tracks. Weyerhaeuser, already a Midwest timber baron, shifted his headquarters to Tacoma, where he built the nation's greatest forest dynasty.

Weyerhaeuser died in 1914, but his heirs built state-of-the-art sawmills and turned the company into a conglomerate. They added steamships, tree farming at the beginning of World War II, and branched into wood pulp, chemicals, and real estate. Clear-cut logging and the invention of new products like plywood and particleboard made pioneer resource use seem child's play. Weyerhaeuser was a model for other wood-products corporations, like Potlatch and Georgia Pacific. Despite post-1960s controversies that swirled around clear-cutting and the export of unsawn logs to Asia (which cost jobs in Northwest sawmills), the corporation continued to grow. By 1999 it owned six million acres in and outside of Washington, and bought Canadian timber giant McMillan-Bloedel. In 2002 it acquired another wood-products firm, Willamette Industries.

THE GOOD EARTH

Harvest crew with horse-drawn combine, 1912.

Rich earth, the kind unfamiliar with the plow, drew settlers to Washington before World War I. Today Washington is one of the top ten farm states. It grows more apples, asparagus, and hops than any part of the country, and harvests much of the nation's wheat, onions, and potatoes. Yet the milk-and-honey vision wasn't as easily fulfilled as pioneers imagined it would be. The gentle Willamette Valley—the Eden that originally inspired the Northwest dream of promised land—was not typical. Even logged-over land around Puget Sound proved less than ideal for many crops. The rich land was east of the Cascades, but there rain was scant. The good ground was separated by scablands, where soils were thin or nonexistent. There was water in the Columbia and Snake, but it ran in coulees, far below surrounding terrain. Nevertheless, farming got a foothold in the Walla Walla Valley in the 1860s, to supply nearby mining camps. There was just enough rain to grow wheat, and in the 1870s wheat spread north to the Palouse Hills. By 1900 the district was the West Coast's biggest grain basket.

On the wheat country's western fringe—straddling the scablands and the voluptuous swells and folds of the Palouse—the McGregor brothers forged a fiefdom that was no booster's mirage. Archie and Peter came to Washington in 1882, searching on foot for a homestead in the Columbia's Big Bend. The area later became an oasis, with water from Grand Coulee Dam. In the 1880s it was bone dry, so the brothers herded sheep for a local rancher, in return for tobacco and a share of the new lambs. The McGregors soon had enough sheep to start their own flock, and grazed it on open range with a million or so other head in the 1880s and 1890s. Overgrazing destroyed native sage and bunchgrass, encouraging invasions of Russian thistle. Overuse and the end of open range pushed the brothers toward farming.

In 1905 they settled in Hooper and founded McGregor Land and Livestock Company. They amassed over 30,000 acres, a third of it suitable for grain, and wheat replaced wool as their prime concern. Before mechanization in the late 1920s the land was reaped by great rigs of horses or mules, up to thirty or more to a team—needed to work the steep slopes. The art of dryland farming saved each drop of soil moisture. The earth was tilled after harvest, to uproot water-thieving weeds. Some land went unsown in alternate years, and it was harrowed relentlessly. The method produced bumper crops, but also big wind and runoff erosion.

In summer, armies of mules and migrant threshers gathered the grain. One man, Joe Ashlock, recalled the work: "A threshing machine, a hot sun that boils the sweat from you in trickling rivulets, seven bathless, shaveless, soapless days with no clean clothing and your blanket roll getting filthier every day." Lenora Torgeson remembered cooking for sixty-four consecutive sixteen-hour days, feeding the crews.

When tractors replaced teams, some farmers mourned the horse-and-mule era. The McGregors weren't so sentimental. What began with "them damned sheep" became after World War II an agribusiness. The family phased out sheep, substituting feedlots that handled 140,000 beef cattle a year. They doubled wheat yields by sowing new strains and using chemical fertilizers, and went into the fertilizer trade themselves. By the 1970s, it added up to a $79 million annual business. By that time, seven men and three air-conditioned combines could harvest more grain than hundreds of men and mules could manage in 1920.

OF FIRE AND FORESTS

The aftermath of early logging, 1902

Gifford Pinchot is not a household name today, but 1.3 million national forest acres in southwest Washington are named for him. The honor is apropos, for Pinchot—along with President Theodore Roosevelt—spurred the breakthrough to a conservation ethic. Gifford Pinchot National Forest is one of eight national forests in the state, covering ten million wood and rangeland acres.

In the early days of commercial lumbering, few voices questioned wanton exploitation. Carl Schurz became U.S. Interior Secretary in the 1870s and urged creation of national forests. The first reserves were mandated by Congress in 1891 while Pinchot, a Connecticut Yankee, was studying forestry in Europe. Returning home, he became head of the Forest Service created by Roosevelt in 1905. The president, a lover of open spaces, added millions of acres to public reserves, despite opposition by many business interests. Yet he and Pinchot were not hostile to commerce. They favored a husbandry approach that protected lands from fire and managed them for human use. Fire, in fact, consumed more trees than logging prior to 1905.

By this time, timber bosses were also ready to think differently. The cut-and-run tactics of pioneer outfits made no sense, once companies started acquiring timberlands of their own. The new era was signaled in 1900 by Weyerhaeuser's purchase of 900,000 acres from railroad king James J. Hill, in the same region where Pinchot's namesake reserve was established. The sale sparked a land rush, and lumbermen were now open to some degree of federal involvement to protect their lands. The Yacolt Burn of 1902 cast searing light on the issue. That inferno consumed 700,000 acres and claimed thirty-five lives.

The marriage of government and corporate profit was sweetened by Pinchot's endorsement of low property taxes for lumbermen, encouraging them to log forests slowly to avoid oversupply. Timber companies were allowed to cut in national forests under permit. Gradually, timber men embraced technocratic forestry, and a forestry school was founded at the University of Washington in 1907. Innovations like plywood and particleboard made use of waste and fire-damaged logs. The paper industry transformed hemlock into a valuable product, and sawdust was recycled as sawmill fuel. The rise of tree farming in the 1940s turned lumbering into an agribusiness. Clear-cut harvesting of old-growth trees exposed wide, sunny lots for monoculture reforestation, where Douglas fir seedlings matured at maximum tempo. Trees were ripe for harvest in forty or fifty years.

Labor conditions were not so rosy. Early loggers floated between flea-ridden forest camps and the skid rows of frontier towns. Unions began organizing them in the 1870s and 1880s, prodding bosses to cut workdays from twelve to ten hours. When timber companies settled down as landowners after 1900, loggers changed as well. They became family men, living in communities near company timberlands and public forests. Yet despite Pinchot's vision of restrained harvests, overcutting created oversupply that depressed wages. When demand nose-dived in the 1930s Depression, half the industry's workers lost their jobs. Some resorted to arson, hoping for work battling the fires they set.

World War II brought an upswing, with its new lumber demands, and the housing boom after 1945 meant more stability for logging towns. Forest products still rank third among Washington's manufacturing sectors. Yet perennial market fluctuations, competition from Canada, the South, and Asian sawmills, and the rise of environmental constraints on harvests meant that forest workers often faced an anxious future.

MOUNTAINEERING ON THE PACIFIC

On Mount Baker's summit, July 3, 1891.

They are a string of volcanic pearls, cascading from Canada's border to the Columbia: Baker (10,778 feet), Glacier Peak (10,568 feet), Rainier (14,411 feet), St. Helens (8,364 feet), and Adams (12,276 feet). The summits are quite climbable. Yet high-country conditions can spin topsy-turvy in minutes, and whiteouts, crevasses, and avalanches are perennial perils.

Early Indians knew this and rarely went above timberline, but gentlemen adventurers relished a risk. Mount Baker was first scaled by English landscape artist Edmund T. Coleman. Foiled in two attempts, Coleman and seven colleagues launched a third try up the Nooksack River from Whatcom on August 4, 1868. Their four Native helpers included Squock, a magician with a river canoe. Coleman's report of the trip blends feelings of piety and struggle redolent of Darwin, Victorian hymnals, and a romantic sense of the sublime. No party member was a seasoned climber, or had even trained for the assault. The Indians stopped before the top, but the others pushed on. Looking down a dizzy 2,000 feet over a vast glacier, Coleman felt the reeling tingle of "Beauty sleeping in the lap of Terror." Fortified by brandy-laced snow water, the troop gained the summit, sang the Doxology, and hoisted Old Glory. Back at Sehome on Bellingham Bay, Coleman wired news of his manly conquest to New York.

Hazard Stevens chafed at Coleman's triumph. Son of Isaac Stevens, Washington Territory's first governor, Hazard bristled to think a dilettante had conquered a Washington patriarch. Setting his sights on Takhoma (Rainier), the "leviathan of mountains," he invited Coleman along to show him up. With Philemon Van Trump, they tramped up the Nisqually River in August 1870, hiring an Indian named Sluiskin to guide them. Coleman soon fell behind and withdrew, whereupon Sluiskin cursed the "worthless Englishman." He and Stevens saw eye-to-eye on that. They differed, though, once they reached snow line, where Sluiskin expected the white men to heed reason and forget the summit. Refusing to budge, Sluiskin warned of snowslides and a demon living atop in a fiery lake. His chanting, punctuated by avalanches, kept them awake long after dark. But Stevens and Van Trump toiled on. Near the top they inched along a precipice that "fell sheer off two thousand feet into a vast abyss." Bracing against gusts at the crest, they waved flags and intoned not a hymn, but three manly cheers.

Twenty years later Fay Fuller became the first woman to reach the summit. Tourism was in full flood, and people debated whether Takhoma (the Nisqually name and Tacoma's choice) should be called Rainier (Seattle's preference). Rainier won out when Congress created a 330,000-acre preserve in 1899—the nation's fifth national park. In 1906 came the founding of The Mountaineers, a club created "to explore, study, preserve, and enjoy the natural beauty of the outdoors." Around 1912, a few members abandoned snowshoes for then-exotic skis, and the club pioneered skiing in the Cascade Mountains. Eddie Bauer discovered skiing in 1921, sold skis in his store, and Austrian and Swiss teachers evangelized downhill techniques in the 1930s. In 1937 the Milwaukee Road opened the Milwaukee Ski Bowl on Snoqualmie Pass. Its weekend ski trains from Seattle, and the use of rope tows on the slopes, inaugurated mass skiing in the state. In 1961, Vashon Island's Bill Kirschner revolutionized skiing when he developed fiberglass skis. So mountaineering on the Pacific, which began with Coleman and Stevens going up, led to millions coming down.

Eddie Bauer ski guide,
1936.

North to Alaska!

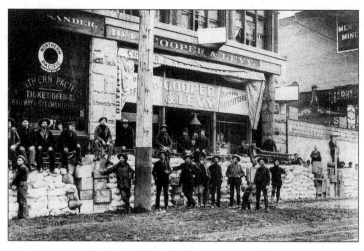

Cooper and Levy Outfitters, Seattle, 1898.

Gold! Gold! Gold! Gold!
Sixty-Eight Rich Men on the Steamer *Portland*
The Steamer Carries $700,000

So proclaimed the *Seattle Post-Intelligencer* as the Portland neared Schwabacher's Dock on July 17, 1897. The truth was even more fabulous. When the ship's golden cargo was weighed, it totaled two tons. Thus began the frenzy of the Klondike gold rush, a stampede that electrified the globe, transformed Seattle, and etched the city on the map of people's minds.

In 1897 and 1898, 100,000 dreamers set out for the Yukon, infected, as Alaska's governor John G. Brady said, by "Klondicitis." Most were greenhorns, ignorant of the hardships ahead and unaware that the best claims were already staked. Many turned back along the way, but 40,000 reached the Klondike. A tiny fraction struck it rich, and even fewer kept their riches. The chief beneficiaries were the Seattle outfitters who catered to the miners' needs.

The main routes went through Alaska's Skagway and Dyea and over White and Chilkoot Passes, but the Klondike itself lay 600 miles beyond in the Canadian interior. To forestall starvation, Canada required each stampeder to bring a year's provisions—a half-ton of flour, clothing, and tools that might cost $500. San Francisco, Portland, and Tacoma competed as staging areas for the stampede, but no city was as close to the goldfields as Seattle, and only Seattle had Erastus Brainerd. Brainerd came West to edit the Seattle Press in 1890. His style was too genteel for the frontier port's readers, but with the gold strike he blossomed as a publicity wizard. Seattle's merchants formed a committee to market their city, with Brainerd as chairman. He beat Seattle's drum in every newspaper across the nation, and sent brochures linking Seattle and the Yukon to European monarchs and South American heads of state. His pamphlet detailing what was needed to become rich in the North and the best way to get there (Seattle!) was distributed by Washington's government.

Brainerd didn't profit from the boom (he died forgotten in Tacoma in 1922), but thousands did. Stores couldn't contain all the supplies, which were piled head-high on the sidewalks. Within six months of the *Portland*'s arrival, firms like Cooper and Levy rang up over $25 million in sales. When the Klondike rush petered out, Seattle's ties to the North remained, for gold was found at Nome in 1898 and in Alaska's interior in 1902. Copper was discovered in 1900, Washington fishermen harvested Alaska's Bristol Bay, and oil was found at Prudhoe Bay in 1968. Seattle was the nerve center for all these rushes.

The Klondike rush doubled Seattle's population to over 80,000 by 1900. In the Alaska-Yukon-Pacific Exposition of 1909, the city celebrated. The extravaganza drew four million visitors. Its boulevard opened southward on a majestic view of Mount Rainier, and the electricity that powered its "Pay Streak" (midway) was ignited when President Taft pushed a button in Washington, D.C. Though Seattle's ties to the North were the focus, hardly less attention was paid to the city's proximity to Hawaii, the Philippines, and Japan. Japanese dignitaries were on the speakers' stand where railroad baron James J. Hill opened the fair before a crowd of 90,000. He symbolized the fair's chief purpose—to attract capital for the region's resources and overseas trade. Brainerd's legacy of boosterism was in the air, as towns vied with slogans to capture the investor's eye, like "Wenatchee, the Land of the Big Red Apple . . . Where Dollars Grow on Trees."

SENSE AND SENSIBILITY

Edward Curtis (far left), 1899, and Asahel Curtis (seated)
atop Mount Shuksan, 1906.

In December 1897, amid the Klondike stampede, the Seattle *Argus* announced the Curtis photography studio intended to "go into the Alaska view business on the most gigantic scale ever attempted." Gold fever produced a boom market for photos of the epic quest, and 29-year-old Edward Curtis meant to profit from it. He didn't plan to go north, however. Instead, he sent his twenty-four-year-old brother, Asahel. Edward stayed behind to manage the business and cultivate his interest in posing local Indians in settings that evoked their vanishing traditions. The decision proved fateful.

Born in Wisconsin, the Curtises moved to Port Orchard, Washington, with their parents in the 1880s. After their father died, Edward opened a Seattle studio in 1892 to support the family. He hired Asahel in 1894, just as photography entered an exciting phase. Negatives produced from gelatin dry-plates turned the craft into a mass-distribution industry. The photogravure process—the chemical transfer of photo images to copper plates, from which luxuriant prints were made—bolstered photography's claim to *art nouveau* status.

Asahel spent two years in the North. Bitten by the gold bug himself, he worked a claim. He found no gold, but discovered the camera's power to create a slice-of-life record of labor and enterprise. Meanwhile, Edward enjoyed a spate of stunning luck. While shooting Mount Rainier he befriended George Bird Grinnell, an authority on

Indian cultures, who asked him to join the 1899 Harriman expedition to Alaska. There Curtis burnished his skills as an outdoor photographer, and Grinnell invited him to witness sun dance rites of Montana's Blackfeet Indians. Thunderstruck by what he saw, Curtis dedicated his life to an obsession: recording Indian folk- and spirit-ways before they disappeared forever.

In a final stroke of fortune, Edward's fine studio portrait of a little girl prompted an invitation to photograph President Teddy Roosevelt's children. He told the president of his Indian project, and TR helped win the support of financier J. P. Morgan for the scheme, called *The North American Indian*. When completed in 1930, it comprised 2,232 images in twenty volumes and twenty portfolios. It was a tour de force.

One cloud darkened Edward's success. Back in 1899, when Asahel returned from the Yukon, he learned that Edward had published some of his gold rush photos in a magazine, claiming credit for the pictures. Edward refused to give Asahel rights to the photos, claiming they belonged to the company. After a lawsuit over the pictures, the brothers hardly spoke to one another again. Though both lived in Seattle, they barred their families from meeting. Edward's Indian pictures earned national fame, but his fixation destroyed his marriage and brought financial ruin before his death in 1952. Today Edward's images arouse mixed emotions. Elegies in sepia ink, they are, in their way, monuments to the dignity of Native people. Yet they are manipulations, reflecting neither real past nor real present.

For a less varnished view of Native life, one looks to Asahel's lens, or that of Frank Matsura, a Japanese-American photographer whose studio was in Okanagan. Asahel's pictures display an artistic touch, but they spring more from business sense than arts-and-crafts sensibility. The younger Curtis was an avid hiker, chairman of Mount Rainier National Park's advisory board, and a founder of The Mountaineers outdoor club. Yet he was also a booster of industry, a promoter of commercial use of public lands, and his reputation was local rather than national. Since his death in 1941 his pictures have been prized testaments of Washington's leap from the frontier to the modern age.

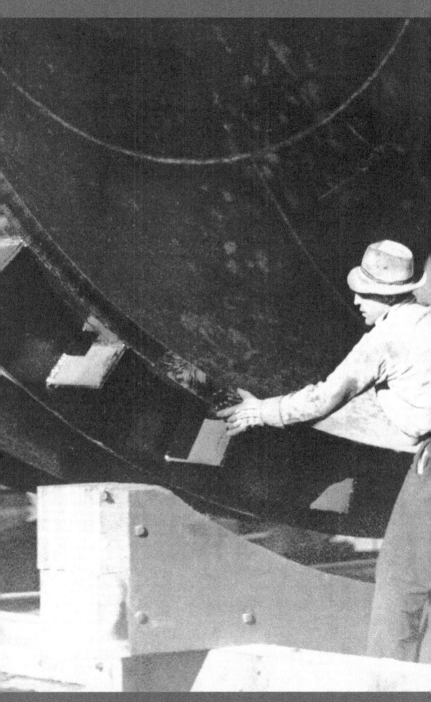

Workmen installing a turbine, Grand Coulee Dam construction site, late 1930s.

THE TWENTIETH CENTURY AND BEYOND

THE WORKMAN'S FRONTIER

Funeral for IWW worker killed in labor-management violence,
Aberdeen, Washington, 1923.

"Womanless, voteless, jobless." So a report described many Washington wage-workers at the end of World War I. Jobless due to boom-and-bust demand for the state's timber and coal. Womanless and voteless since so many were rootless transients, riding the rails with a bedroll, rarely settling to cast a ballot. Yet the region, one of them declared, was "Mecca in the dreams of the misguided worker. . . . If I can only get West has been his only thought." The gap between dream and reality spawned social unrest.

Few laws governed labor relations. In an age of rock-jawed individualism, opportunity was not a thing to take, but to seize. That meant a war for wealth, or a share of it. Tacoma produced the first explosion, and it had a nasty racist taint. There the Knights of Labor organized coal, railroad, and forest workers to improve wages and working conditions. They persuaded bosses to cut the timber workday from twelve to ten hours and advocated votes for women and a progressive income tax. But their notion of raising pay included driving out the Chinese. In 1885 workmen held torchlight parades, bearing banners exhorting "Discharge your Chinese." On a rainy November 3, vigilantes entered the Chinese district, ordering its 700 residents to "pack up at once." They were driven to the tracks and onto the next train to Portland. Four to six died and the district was torched. Seattle spawned a similar riot months later.

The Knights faded from class warfare's stage, to be replaced by the AFL and the Industrial Workers of the World (IWW)—the "Wobblies" of radical legend. The Wobblies were homespun Marxists who rejected racism, and they opened their ranks to all toilers. Romantic rebels, they spurned compromise. Their first success was in Spokane, in a "free speech fight" during 1909–10. There they declared war on the "sharks"—labor contractors who defrauded workers by taking their money with promises of nonexistent jobs. Ignoring a city ban on street oratory, they denounced the sharks while chained to lampposts. The cost of jailing hundreds over five months forced the city to concede, and the sharks' business permits were canceled.

Success emboldened the Wobblies and boosted their fame. But their turning point came in Everett in November 1916, when they stepped into a shingle weavers' strike that was about to fail. Using the free speech tactic, a group of forty were jailed by police, then beaten and driven from town. Outraged, about 250 Wobblies—some armed—sailed north from Seattle on the steamship *Verona*. Everett's sheriff and deputies were waiting. When the *Verona* tied up someone fired a shot, and the battle was on. Several Wobblies jumped overboard and drowned or were shot in the water. When the smoke cleared five Wobblies were dead or dying, and 31 were wounded. Two deputies were killed and twenty were wounded. Seventy-four Wobblies were charged with murder. They won acquittal, and the IWW survived to lead other strikes as late as 1932. Yet it never fully recovered from the "Everett Massacre." A telling blow occurred in Centralia on November 11, 1919, when American Legion men, celebrating the anniversary of the end of World War I, attacked the hall of the pacifist Wobblies. Four legionnaires were fatally wounded by Wobbly fire. Several Wobs were arrested, and that night a mob hanged a Wobbly named Wesley Everest from a bridge. A jury found eight Wobs guilty of second-degree murder and they received long jail terms. The lynching was never punished.

Boeing and
the Aviation Revolution

William Boeing (right) with mail and Boeing "C" seaplane, 1919.

On March 21, 2001, three weeks after an earthquake rattled their state, Washingtonians awoke to another shock: Boeing was shifting its headquarters to another part of the country. Most operations of the airplane manufacturer would stay in Seattle's environs, where the company started in 1916 and where it was Washington's largest employer. But its nerve center would go—plus 1,000 jobs. The notice jolted regional pride and stirred memories of the "Boeing bust" of 1971. That tremor, with its thousands of layoffs, inspired a Pacific Highway billboard: "Will the last person leaving SEATTLE— Turn out the lights."

The company began as a rich timberman's passion. William E. Boeing, son of a Michigan lumber baron, came to Grays Harbor and made millions in the forest industry. Viewing an air show in 1910, he was smitten by aviation's romance. He learned to fly, built his first plane in 1916, and created Pacific Aero Products—renamed the Boeing Airplane Company in 1917. The fledgling firm enjoyed instant success thanks to World War I contracts for trainer planes, but hovered near bankruptcy when demand collapsed in 1919. Its breakthrough came after 1925, when the Kelly Act enabled private firms to bid for lucrative airmail contracts.

The newly christened Boeing System began service in 1927, with the open-cockpit Model 40 biplane. The larger, enclosed Model 80A Trimotor debuted in 1928, with space for mail, eighteen passengers, and registered nurses to serve them—the first stewardesses. The company burgeoned, merging with firms like Pacific Air Transport and Wichita's Stearman. Boeing flexed his corporate muscle, threatening to move to Los Angeles if he didn't get a new airfield, and got his wish when King County dedicated Boeing Field in 1928. His conglomerate, christened United Aircraft and Transport in 1929, reached its zenith in 1930–31 when the Post Office awarded the nation's key mail routes to three aviation giants: American, TWA, and Boeing's United. To celebrate, engineers designed the all-metal Model 247—the nation's first true airliner, able to fly coast-to-coast in twenty hours. But the United conglomerate was assailed as a monopoly in congressional hearings. Ensuing antitrust laws denied airplane makers the right to postal routes, and forced the breakup of Boeing's holding company. Humiliated and irate, Boeing sold his company shares and played no further part in the firm's destiny.

The company lived on and soared in World War II when, with its rival, Douglas Aviation, it became the chief builder of military aircraft. Boeing's B-17 bomber was the most famous war bird of the era, and its B-29 was also a legend. In 1947 Boeing adapted German swept-wing designs to produce the first jet bomber, and launched another revolution when the first passenger jet—the 707—rolled out in 1954. In a heart-throbbing display at the 1955 Gold Cup boat races on Lake Washington, test pilot Tex Johnson demonstrated the 707's maneuverability by rolling the huge bird *twice* at an altitude of 500 feet. The impromptu maneuver sealed the plane's success—and that of its 727, 737, and 747 descendants, rolled out in the 1960s. With its head start in jet propulsion, Boeing surpassed Douglas, even buying the firm in 1997. It surged into the space age, as well, with its Saturn V booster that took *Apollo 11* astronauts to the moon in 1969. With tens of thousands of employees still in the Evergreen State, even the transfer of firm headquarters to Chicago is unlikely to alter the adage "As Boeing goes, so goes Washington."

THE WASHINGTON STATE FERRIES

The ferry Kalakala *on Elliot Bay, July 5, 1935.*

Alaska's Kodiak Island was the scene of a strange salvage operation in 1997–98. There, workers dislodged the carcass of the 276-foot *Kalakala*—once-proud flagship of Washington's ferries—from tons of backfill that surrounded it for twenty-five years. Conceived in 1934, the *Kalakala* was, in the apt words of its rescuers, "yesterday's vision of tomorrow." From the mid-'30s to the mid-'60s the *Kalakala* was a celebrity—an art-deco counterpart to railroading's *Super Chief* streamliners and the spaceships of Buck Rogers fantasy. But its plunge from stardom was swift. In 1966 the vessel was replaced on the Seattle–Bremerton run by the new *Hyak*. Sold to fish packers in 1967, it was towed to Alaska, interred on Kodiak in 1972, and converted to a shrimp processing plant. Its excavation, its Seattle homecoming behind a tug in 1998, and proposed restoration triggered memories of the history of ferries in the Evergreen State.

Before 1900, people traveled Puget Sound via independently owned steamboats. The Model-T changed all that, and by 1930 car ferries were king. One company—the Black Ball Line owned by Captain Alexander Peabody—gained a near monopoly on ferry traffic. In the 1930s Peabody bought fourteen surplus ferries in San Francisco, including the burnt-out hull of the Peralta, which he rebuilt into the futuristic *Kalakala*—the "silver bullet" or "silver slug," depending on one's taste. Yet all was not well. The Depression energized organized labor, and Peabody had several run-ins with unions. World War II brought a lull in labor-management discord as everyone pitched in to win the fight. Ferry ridership mushroomed between Seattle and the shipyards of Bremerton—especially aboard the 2,000-passenger *Kalakala*, which (despite the sleek silhouette) shook tremendously. The vessel was also bad-luck prone. In 1936 it smashed into the ferry *Chippewa*, which lost five cars, and it rammed its terminal numerous times.

The war's end meant nationwide rejoicing, but trouble for Washington ferries. Ridership dipped as shipbuilding declined, Black Ball hiked fares 10 percent to meet rising costs, and unions blustered as Peabody held tight on working hours and wages. When he proposed a 30 percent fare increase in 1947, the ferries became a political storm center. The increase was temporarily approved by the state, subject to a review of ferry operations. In the meantime, a six-day strike dealt a crushing blow to commuters, caught behind the eight ball of rate hikes and between the scissors of labor shutdowns. After reviewing the situation, the state ordered a rollback of Peabody's fare increase to 10 percent, and the outraged captain had to refund the difference to passengers. In February 1948, he suspended service for ten days.

By this time, people of all political hues were contemplating alternatives: a string of cross-Sound bridges, a public ferry line to compete with Peabody, or a state buyout of Black Ball. The buyout scheme won. Just before New Year's 1950, Governor Arthur Langlie announced the state would buy most of Peabody's fleet, which it did for $4.9 million. On June 1, 1951, the state ferries began operation as a public utility. Considering the troubles of the late 1940s, it has been reasonably smooth sailing ever since—despite periodic cost overruns and accidents. Washington operates the world's largest ferry system and its millions of riders pay roughly the same fares—allowing for inflation—that passengers did in 1951. The vessels, mostly bearing Indian names and decked out in signature green and white, are also among the state's top tourist draws. As for the *Kalakala*, funds couldn't be found to restore it and it was demolished in 2015. Kirkland, its launchpoint in 1934, plans to create public art from its rusty scraps.

MIXED BLESSING:
TAMING THE COLUMBIA

LEFT: *Officials viewing Grand Coulee Dam Site, October 14, 1937.*
RIGHT: *Puget Power advertisement, about 1970.*

—Into each detail of the construction has gone the painstaking foresight which has made the finished project everything desired by man.

—White man's dams mean no more salmon.

These two opinions met head-on in the 1940s. The first appeared in a souvenir booklet extolling the new Grand Coulee Dam. The second reflected an Indian chief's suspicions of a lack of foresight in taming the Columbia. Both were exaggerations, yet each held part of the truth.

The aboriginal Columbia was a navigator's nightmare. Plunging 2,600 feet in its course from Canada's Rockies to the Pacific, it gushed over or through 109 hazards with names like Death Rapids and Hell's Gate. In the name of irrigation, electricity, and flood control, engineers turned it into a string of lakes in forty years. Today there are fourteen high dams between the Columbia's headwaters and its mouth.

The Army Corps of Engineers threw the first loop around the river's neck in 1933, when it began Bonneville Dam, forty miles east of Portland. The project was approved by President Roosevelt to generate jobs and electricity, and to repay local congressmen for their support. Bonneville's sixty-five-foot-high spillway and powerhouse were finished in 1939, at a cost of $88 million. The dam boasted the world's then-largest shiplock, and fish ladders to aid salmon swimming upstream to spawn.

Bonneville was dwarfed by $300 million Grand Coulee, built at a canyon bend ninety-five miles northwest of Spokane. Conceived by local boosters and the Bureau of Reclamation, more for irrigation than for electric power, the scheme's idea was simple yet bold. Water backed up at the 550-foot dam would be pumped 280 feet to the canyon's south rim, where it would flow down into Grand Coulee, a dry fifty-mile trough cut by ancient floods. The arroyo would become a tank for gravity-fed capillary canals to water the scablands to the south. Work commenced in 1933, and soon 7,000 toilers were engaged. The last concrete was poured in December 1941, when news of Pearl Harbor jolted the nation. Skeptics who once doubted the project's value praised its wisdom, for power from Grand Coulee and its Bonneville sibling built the aluminum, aviation, and atomic industries that helped win World War II.

The project's original reclamation purpose was realized in the 1950s. Water from the dam's pumps first flowed into Grand Coulee in 1951, and soon over half a million acres blossomed—fortified by fertilizers and pesticides. A vision was realized, but the natural river was gone and it was mainly corporate agribusiness that made the desert bloom, not a host of yeoman farmers.

Meanwhile, wild salmon and steelhead migrated upriver to breed, but in far fewer numbers than before. A host of factors caused the decline: overfishing, silt from logging, and chemical pollution. The dams were a prime cause, though, for countless spawning pools vanished beneath reservoirs. The estimated ten to sixteen million wild chinook and sockeye that once ran the Columbia plunged to a few hundred thousand, to be replaced by disease-prone hatchery fish. And for the hatchlings, swimming to sea through hydro turbines was akin to a gauntlet of mammoth food processors. Some made it through, but many were barged or trucked around the dams in tanks. Their returning numbers, in any case, were about 15 percent of aboriginal runs. The old chief's fears of a salmon apocalypse may have been premature, but there was no doubt the ancient river culture of his people—based on salmon abundance—was now but a memory.

A Desert Transformed

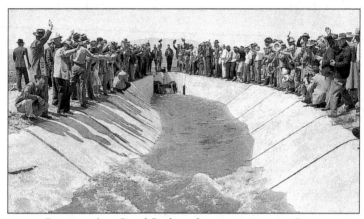

First water from Grand Coulee reclamation project, near Pasco.

Traveling west in 1894, New Yorker Kirk Munroe groaned that "for dust, glare, heat, and dreary monotony of scenery, a mid-summer ride through that section of Eastern Washington traversed by the Northern Pacific is unsurpassed by any other portion of the Great American Desert." Yet Munroe saw a miracle at Yakima. "The ripple of running waters was in the air," he enthused. "Every house in town stands . . . embowered by fruit trees, in yards green with grass or gay with a riotous growth of roses." The marvel was wrought by adding water from the Yakima River, via the new Sunnyside Canal.

Sunnyside was one of many pioneer efforts to make the desert an oasis. Few were so successful. Many were financed by speculators who aimed to drive up land values. Once property was sold, they couldn't be counted on to keep providing water. The dream of an Eden in the entire Columbia Basin was not realized until the federal Grand Coulee reclamation project became operational in the 1950s. Even before Grand Coulee, though, irrigation worked wonders in places. The sun-kissed fruit Munroe saw in Yakima foreshadowed the orchards of Wenatchee and the Yakima Valley.

At Wenatchee, a mix of water, long summer days, and crisp autumns was just the recipe for apples. James J. Hill promoted orchards there, to create business for his Great Northern Line. He platted a town in the 1890s, and improved existing ditches to divert water from the Wenatchee River. By 1904 the town had 4,000 people, and by 1910 Washington was America's leading apple state. Wenatchee's success lay as much in marketing as husbandry. The Red Delicious variety was so adroitly promoted that it shaped our image of what an apple should be.

With water from Grand Coulee after World War II, combined with fertilizers and pesticides, the Columbia Basin burst forth with peaches, potatoes, hops, and alfalfa. There was, of course, a downside. In 1947, government scientists praised DDT, marveling that "its effect lasts, sometimes as long as a year!" Decades later the toxin had to be banned.

But the big surprise was wine. Munroe noticed grapes in Yakima, but they were Concords, not the *Vitis vinifera* of European vintages. Outside California and New York, wine before the 1960s was something most Americans deemed distinctly plebian, best sold by the jug. In the 1970s, though, America's thirst for good wine soared. Washington's tiny industry bordered on collapse in 1969, but pioneers like Washington State University's Walter Clore paved the way for a premium wine industry. Working at stations in Walla Walla and Prosser, Clore planted an array of vines to see which would thrive.

Clore was originally interested in grape juice, but in the 1950s his aide Vere Brummund began making wine with varietal grapes. Brummund converted Clore to the cult of Bacchus, along with biologist Charles Nagel and chemist George Carter. Nagel made the first wines at Pullman in 1964, and started a tasting program. From this came a report that became a beacon of Washington viticulture. It showed, as someone said, that south-central Washington was "the Mediterranean turned upside down"—able to balance the fullness of south European wines with the acidic intensity of northern vintages. By 1972, when Seattle investor Wally Opdycke bought a small *vinifera* vineyard, the confidence existed to spur an industry. With an infusion of money by U.S. Tobacco, Opdycke's Ste. Michelle Rieslings won prizes in California and restaurant contracts in New York. Other risk-takers jumped on the bandwagon, and vineyards sprouted in the Yakima, Columbia, and Walla Walla Valleys. Today, experts recognize fourteen distinct wine-growing regions in Washington. With 50,000 acres of vineyards and nearly 1,000 wineries, the state trails only California in U.S. wine production, and its Rieslings, Cabs, and Merlots enjoy global esteem.

WORLD WAR II:
THE STATE IN A CRUCIBLE

Celebrating war's end, Seattle, 1945.

No era was as pivotal to Washington's shift to the center of national life than World War II. From aviation's growth, to shipbuilding, aluminum smelting, and atomic power's birth at Hanford, the comet of war swept the state along in its tail.

Washingtonians feared enemy invasion. Antisubmarine nets were strung in Puget Sound, and the roofs of Boeing's Seattle plant were disguised as a sleepy suburbia, similar to a movie set. Boeing's expansion epitomized the war's impact. British orders for its B-17 boosted its payroll from 4,000 to 10,000, even before America entered the war. In 1943 it rolled out the larger B-29, and began recruiting women workers nationwide. By 1944 its Seattle area plants employed 50,000, nearly half women. At peak production, Boeing's swing shifts rolled out sixteen B-17s a day, and six B-29s besides. To feed Boeing's need for aluminum, refineries mushroomed in the Portland–Vancouver area, powered by electricity from Bonneville and Grand Coulee Dams. Shipyards hummed, forestry and farming boomed, and the armed forces bought all the salmon the state could can.

War enterprise meant a swell in human numbers, from 1.7 million residents in 1940 to 2.4 million by 1950. The state's population profile changed, as well. Japanese-Americans in its western counties were branded "enemy aliens" and sent to internment camps. Few questioned the injustice. Meanwhile, African-Americans came as servicemen and workers in defense industries. Though some of Washington's pioneers were black—starting with William Clark's slave York—its black population had always been small. Now some of its towns grew sizable black neighborhoods, and the state's black population increased from 7,000 in 1940 to 30,000 in 1950. Hispanic workers came, as well. Thousands of field hands were recruited from Mexico, to tend Eastern Washington's crops.

The rush of newcomers aroused racial tensions. Labor unions at Boeing denied membership to black workers. Businesses from Bremerton to Walla Walla refused to serve black and Hispanic servicemen and workers. In one incident, black soldiers at Seattle's Fort Lawton rioted when they thought Italian war prisoners were treated better than they were by the army and businesses. Seattle Mayor William Devin's multiracial Civic Unity Committee tried to foster harmony between ethnic communities, helping create a climate for passage of the state's Law Against Discrimination in Employment in 1949. Such trends, set in motion during the war, slowly altered patterns of discrimination. Eventually—in Spokane's James Chase, Pasco's Joe Jackson, Yakima's Henry Beauchamp, Seattle's Norm Rice, and Tacoma's Harold Moss—cities elected black mayors in the 1980s and 1990s, and Charles Z. Smith became a state supreme court justice.

Amid the war in 1943, Washington Secretary of State Belle Reeves observed that "No state has been more profoundly affected economically by the expansion of war industries than Washington." She was right. Seattle was one of three cities that led in per capita award of defense contracts. Yet despite the growth, the sense of purpose, and the joy when it was over, the war's climax evokes complex feelings today. It came when a Boeing-built B-29 dropped an atomic bomb on Nagasaki, armed by radioactive explosives refined at Hanford.

People feared the economic bubble would burst when the war ended, but defense still fueled growth as the Cold War followed victory over Germany and Japan. Building on its leap forward as a military contractor, aviation replaced lumbering as the state's biggest industry. Even so, the postwar housing boom spurred the forest industry to new heights. And Hanford's role grew in the anxious climate of the superpowers' race for nuclear dominance.

THE JAPANESE INTERNMENT

Japanese-American girl awaiting internment, Bellingham, Washington, 1942.

> *Over the horizon of the wide Pacific,*
> *Entertaining high ambitions,*
> *I looked for eternal happiness,*
> *Great love . . .*
> *Huge efforts . . .*
> *Large land . . .*
> *Vast sky . . .*
> *I survey my future path.*

Armed with such dreams, railroad worker Kenji Abe departed his Japanese home to settle in distant Pullman, Washington, in 1906. He was one of thousands of Japanese men who sought work in the Northwest at the start of a new century. The low-paying jobs they took, once performed by Chinese, were freed up by America's Chinese exclusion laws of the 1880s. Other Japanese followed to serve the workers' needs, branching into retail commerce and truck gardening. By World War I, one-fifth of Washington's cannery workers were Japanese. Japanese section hands helped build the Stevens Pass Tunnel, and others fostered the shell fishery by importing oyster stock from Japan. They made their mark above all in agriculture, establishing farms in Western Washington, the Yakima Valley, and around Spokane. During World War I, up to 70 percent of Seattle's Pike Place Market stalls were run by Japanese gardeners.

Like others from Asia, Japanese were often viewed with suspicion as aliens and rivals for jobs. A 1908 agreement with Japan banned further labor immigration to the United States. Yet unlike the Chinese, Japanese men already resident in America could still bring wives to join them—at least until 1924. The result was the birth of second and third generations of Japanese heritage, known respectively as Nisei and Sansei. Citizens by American birth, the Nisei were nonetheless reckoned foreign by many non-Asians. Such prejudice spawned a federal law in 1924, banning all new immigration from Asia except the Philippines. It also declared all Asian-born American residents ineligible for citizenship. To combat such legislation, Japanese leaders formed the Japanese Association, with branches across the state.

Their American dream was shattered by imperial Japan's infamous attack of December 7, 1941. In the panic following Pearl Harbor, ethnic Japanese were redefined as enemy aliens. On February 19, 1942, President Roosevelt issued Executive Order 9066, deporting West Coast residents of Japanese heritage to internment camps, mostly in the nation's interior. Two-thirds of the deportees were U.S. citizens. The first column of detainees filed aboard a ferry at Bainbridge Island, Washington, in the pale light of March 30, 1942, bound for Manzanar in the California desert. A few outcasts challenged the relocation's legality—most famously the college student Gordon Hirabayashi. They were overruled on grounds of military necessity, a verdict upheld by the Supreme Court.

The deportees suffered barbed-wire incarceration and humiliation; they lost their jobs, and in some cases their assets. Yet Nisei and Sansei men were permitted to volunteer for military duty, and many served with distinction in combat. After the war, Japanese-Americans had to rebuild. Gradually the climate changed. The McCarran–Walter Act of 1952 reversed the Asian exclusion act of 1924, declaring race illegal as a basis for immigration law, and the civil rights movement grew in the 1960s. In the 1980s, judicial rulings overturned Gordon Hirabayashi's wartime conviction for resisting internment, and in 1988 Congress apologized for treatment of Japanese-Americans during the war and awarded $20,000 to each victim. Japanese-Americans now form Washington's largest Asian-American community.

THE STORY OF HANFORD

Nuclear reactor at Hanford Reservation and Columbia River.

Army leaders and Du Pont engineers made the decision around Christmas, 1942. The nation's first large-scale nuclear reactor would be built near the towns of Hanford and White Cliffs, in Washington's Columbia Basin. Stretching northeast from the Rattlesnake Hills, the site seemed ideal. Remote, thinly peopled, yet near railroads and on the Columbia, it promised ample water to cool the reactor, and electricity from Grand Coulee Dam. The project's top-secret goal was the production of plutonium to fuel a new weapon to speed victory over Germany and Japan. Urgency spurred the undertaking. The physics of unlocking the atom's power were broadly understood by elite scientists, as Albert Einstein told President Roosevelt in 1939. Amid total war, it seemed only a matter of time before one nation unleashed a bomb.

Once the decision was made, things moved swiftly. The 1,500 residents of the 640-square-mile area received eviction notices, and 51,000 construction laborers converged on the site. The village of Richland mushroomed, serving as site headquarters for the Hanford phase of the now-famous Manhattan Project—the crash program to create an atomic bomb. Sustained by 16,000 packs of cigarettes a day and 12,000 gallons of beer per week, the construction army took twenty-eight months to build the B Reactor, and it was started by physicist Enrico Fermi on September 26, 1944. Months later Hanford plutonium powered the first atomic test in New Mexico, and then fueled the Fat Man bomb released on Nagasaki on August 9, 1945, ending the war with a blast equal to 21,000 tons of TNT.

That was the first chapter of Hanford's story. An arms race with Russia followed World War II, inflating the demand for atomic power. Meanwhile, optimists prophesied peacetime uses, while pacifists preached a "ban the bomb" message in the 1950s. In the Cold War setting, Hanford enjoyed several new growth spurts. Ultimately, nine reactors were constructed. Peak production occurred between 1957 and 1963, capped by President Kennedy's visit in 1963—shortly before his assassination—to dedicate the new N Reactor and herald his intent to close the missile gap with Russia.

Looking back, Hanford's role in America's victory in World War II and the Cold War is indisputable, yet its legacy remains disturbingly mixed. The contamination hazard, though recognized from the start, was gravely misjudged. At first, some wastes were dumped on the soil, where they contaminated the water table through seepage. Water was pumped back into the Columbia as radioactive effluent. There were leaks in many disposal tanks, dust from the site's powdery soil carried radioactive particulates, and the area became a dump for other nuclear sites. Escalating fears concerning these wastes, coupled with Russia's Chernobyl nuclear disaster, put the last military reactor—Kennedy's N reactor—on cold standby in 1988, and shut it down in 1991.

Project directors candidly explain their present mission as the "largest waste cleanup effort in world history." Underground tanks containing millions of gallons of hazardous wastes continue to leak, awaiting the long-delayed completion of a safe storage plant to contain the material until its radioactivity dissipates over hundreds of thousands of years. Reports of airborne contamination spreading miles from the site erode public confidence in cleanup methods. There may be a silver strand, though, behind the toxic cloud. Hanford's operations kept agribusiness out, conserving much of the reserve as a time capsule of indigenous shrub-steppe habitat. In June 2000, President Clinton created the 200,000-acre Hanford Reach National Monument to protect the last untamed stretch of the Columbia and its splendid White Cliffs, ironically preserved by the off-limits secrecy of the Hanford Project. In 2009 authorities even allowed public tours of the B Reactor, which later became part of the Manhattan Project National Historical Park created in 2014.

Go East, Young Man!

William O. Douglas as head of the federal Securities and Exchange Commission, late 1930s.

"We'll see," said President Roosevelt in 1939 when one of his key aides, William O. Douglas, planned to resign to be dean of Yale's law school. Weeks later FDR nominated Douglas to the Supreme Court. On April 17, Douglas took his seat on the tribunal—at forty, the second-youngest justice ever appointed. When he retired thirty-six years later, the man from Yakima had served longer than any previous judge.

Born in Minnesota in 1898, Douglas grew up in central Washington. A minister's son, his father died when he was six, and his mother settled in Yakima. The Douglases lived on the wrong side of the tracks, and he worked at any job he could find. An early bout with polio prompted his lifelong love of hiking and fishing. The outdoors, he believed, helped vanquish the disease, and he repaid it by embracing a preservationist ethic.

As a teenager Douglas hated the feeling that rich people looked down their noses at him, and his anger spurred an affinity for the outsider. In his autobiography *Go East Young Man*, he recalled how a prudish businessman once hired him as a naive "stool pigeon" to ferret out prostitutes and bootleggers in Yakima's skid row, then report them to the law. He soon discovered more sympathy for street people than for stuffy hypocrites. A scholarship enabled Douglas to attend Whitman College. Afterward he taught high school in Yakima for two years, but his sights were set on the law. He entered Columbia Law School, where he finished second in his class. By the 1930s he had a top reputation in bankruptcy law—a booming trade after the Wall Street crash.

In 1936 Douglas was named to FDR's Securities and Exchange Commission. With his brilliance, humble roots, and passion, he was tailor-made for the New Deal. He played the blunt westerner's role, with his salty speech, tousled hair, and rumpled suits. But underneath, the common man from Yakima reinvented himself as an East Coast insider. By 1937 he was head of the SEC, a member of FDR's poker circle, and the president's preferred bartender, having mastered the dry martini that Roosevelt loved. Both men's triumph over polio was surely important, too.

On the Supreme Court, Douglas was first known as a business law expert. During World War II he twice voted with the court majority to uphold incarceration of Japanese-Americans as "enemy aliens." Maybe that mistake spurred his later zeal to stretch the span of civil liberties, for in the 1950s he gained fame as a radical in his judicial opinions—though now many of them are part of the legal mainstream. Douglas wrote the court's disputed 1949 opinion, affirming a person's right to expression even if it "brings about . . . unrest or creates a disturbance." No strict observer of the separation of powers, he endorsed judicial activism in shaping law in accord with reform agendas. His positions opposing censorship and religion in public schools, and supporting desegregation, women's rights, and protections for the accused, made him the most controversial justice.

Judicial robes did not deter him from attacking Vietnam policy in the 1960s, or predicting the government's overthrow if it ignored activist criticisms. Douglas's private life also ruffled feathers, for he divorced three wives and married four; the last two were forty years his junior. Following a stroke he resigned the bench in 1975, reminisced at his Goose Prairie retreat, and died in 1980. His best epitaph was coined by L. A. Powe Jr., a historian of First Amendment rights: "he broke the mold."

Not So Benign Nature

Night eruption of Mount St. Helens, Paul Kane, 1847.

Washington—at least its western part—is famous for its lack of seasonal excess. "The pleasantest winter I ever spent was a summer on Puget Sound," Mark Twain remarked. Still, the state is sometimes a stage for extremes. Wynoochee-Oxbow on the Olympic Peninsula recorded 184.56 inches of rain in 1931, still a record for the Lower 48 states. With 1,124 inches of snow in 1998–99, Mount Baker's Heather Meadows surpassed the world record for snowfall, held before by Mount Rainier. Every six years or so, the Yakima and Columbia Valleys endure winters that give winegrowers a scare. Even on the Cascades' west slope, Nor'Easters from Canada can plunge winter windchills to –25°F. The Columbus Day Storm, the state's worst recorded tempest, occurred in 1962. Sweeping in from the Philippines, winds clocked 160 miles an hour on Washington's southwest coast.

Earthquakes and volcanic eruptions are the best-known Northwest extremes. Though not to California's extent, Washington is earthquake country. Over 1,000 tremors are recorded each year, though most go unnoticed. Yet big quakes do occur several times per century. They are caused mainly by subduction of the state's coast: the eastward movement of the offshore Juan de Fuca tectonic plate, 3 to 4 centimeters per year, under the landward North American plate. Geologists believe a giant quake occurred about 900 A.D. that lifted Alki Point twelve feet. Another happened sixty miles offshore around 1700, causing a thirty-three-foot sea wave and dropping the outer coast six feet. The strongest jolt in the past 200 years—magnitude 7.4—occurred in 1872 near Lake Chelan, causing a landslide that briefly dammed the Columbia. Most threatening to brick and mortar were recent tremors centered near Olympia in 1949 (7.1) and 2001 (6.8) and Seattle-Tacoma in 1965 (6.5).

The shock that riveted the world was the explosion of Mount St. Helens in 1980. Youngest of the Cascade volcanoes, St. Helens was first studied by the Navy's Wilkes expedition in 1841. The peak erupted often from 1800 to 1857, and in 1847 artist Paul Kane painted an enchanting view of eight Indians watching a fiery blast on its flank from a canoe on the Cowlitz. After 1857 the mountain slept for a hundred years. But geologists grew wary as they studied the mountain's past, and in 1975 experts cautioned it might erupt "before the end of the century."

On March 20, 1980, a magnitude 4.2 tremor heralded the mountain's intent to shake. Over the next two months small spasms shook its north slope, ash and steam rose from its crown, and an eerie bulge materialized near its summit. May 18 dawned sunny, and at 7 a.m. volcanologist David Johnston observed no alarming change in the summit's behavior. Then, at 8:32 a.m., the bulge collapsed and the north face exploded, sending a lightning-fringed cloud of gas and ash twelve miles high. Ashen skies caused darkness at noon in Yakima and Spokane, ash fell as far away as Oklahoma, and Interstate 90 from Spokane to Seattle was closed for a week. The blast turned trees for nineteen miles around into ghostly pickup sticks, and mudslides surged down the Toutle River, clogging Columbia shipping channels. Johnston and fifty-six others were killed, mainly by asphyxiation. Despite the explosion's human cost, the fact that it happened in bright daylight aided science. It was clearly observed, and has become history's most carefully studied eruption.

Scoop and Maggie

U.S. *Senators Henry M. Jackson (left) and Warren G. Magnuson.*

A "1000 per cent New Dealer"; "last of the red-hot cold warriors"—
the labels say a lot, respectively, about Warren G. Magnuson and
Henry M. "Scoop" Jackson, the duo who ruled Washington's
congressional politics from FDR to Reagan. Democrats, both were
popular with many Republicans. The clout they brandished in "the
other Washington" (D.C.) make them twins in voters' memories,
though their personalities were studies in contrast. The difference is
captured in a cartoon found in Jackson's papers. In it, the fun-loving
Magnuson counsels: "You've got a great career in politics ahead of
you, Jackson, if you'll only stop telling the truth."

Magnuson was an orphan, born of unknown parents in 1905.
Adopted by a Minnesota banker, he worked as a teenager on
threshing gangs and played high-school quarterback. From the start
he was known for his chiseled good looks, hard drinking, and way
with the ladies. In the 1920s he rode boxcars to Seattle and worked
his way through law school at the University of Washington. Elected
to the state legislature in 1932, he embraced the Democrats' welfare
agenda. In 1936 he rode FDR's coattails to the U.S. House of
Representatives as a loyal soldier of the New Deal, and Washingtonians
sent him to the Senate in 1944.

A political natural, Maggie built a capitol career that lasted until 1980, when he was unseated by Republican Slade Gorton. For years he chaired the Senate's commerce and appropriations committees, where he championed Medicare, consumer safeguards, and scientific research, but he never became a national name. He flourished as a pork-barrel politician, looking out for the Evergreen State's special interests—labor, aviation, hydroelectric and nuclear power, fisheries, agribusiness, and shipping. As appropriations chairman, joked Walter Mondale, he divided federal dollars evenly: "half for Washington State and half for the rest of the country."

If anything, Jackson became more adept than Maggie at forging special-interest alliances. At his peak, friend and foe called him "the senator from Boeing." He hated the tag, and under their humor even rivals respected his straight-arrow integrity. Born in Everett in 1912, his nickname "Scoop" came from a sister: he reminded her of a comic-strip character of that name. Like Maggie, Scoop worked his way through UW law school and succumbed to the hex of politics. A nonsmoker and infrequent drinker, his notion of fun was a game of Ping-Pong. In 1940, having assailed Everett's gambling dens and brothels as Snohomish County Attorney, he was elected to the House of Representatives, and he joined Maggie in the Senate in 1952.

Named to Joe McCarthy's subcommittee on government operations, he made a splash protesting McCarthy's allegations of communism in the army and State Department—though he'd used "soft on communism" in his Senate campaign. He made his mark as an anti-Soviet hawk on defense issues. In 1960 he came within a hair of being John Kennedy's running mate, and never forgave Jack for choosing LBJ. Scoop defended Vietnam policy under LBJ and Nixon, and the Pentagon had no firmer friend. While working with Maggie to promote Washington's interests, Scoop forged foreign policy alliances on both sides of the senatorial aisle, and championed Israel's security to stop the Mideast spread of Soviet power. By the '70s sober Scoop stood so tall that he twice cast his hat into the presidential primary ring—without success. Undeterred, he was going strong in 1983 when, back from a China trip, he died in Everett. Magnuson followed six years later.

THE BOLDT DECISION

*Colville stick game, "Ceremony of Tears," 1939,
before Kettle Falls salmon fishery was flooded by Grand Coulee Dam.*

Before non-Natives came to Washington, Indians had evolved an array of tools and traditions for living, from the dry plateau to the rainy coast. Indian life was not one thing, but many. Yet reliance on salmon was a widespread bond, and Native cultures were not mental worlds apart. It was otherwise when it came to Indians and settlers. Indians understood tribal rights to land and resource use, but—unlike non-Native newcomers—did not view soil as a commodity and property as individual legal title. From the settlers' perspective, Natives didn't till the soil and so had little right to it.

To make way for farms, treaties shunted Indians to reservations in the 1850s. Governor Isaac Stevens's covenants promised Natives education and the freedom to fish and hunt off-reservation in their "usual and accustomed grounds and stations." Yet Indians were not citizens under federal law, only government wards. It was 1924 before most Natives received American citizenship. Meanwhile, reservations were diminished by laws permitting sale of Indian land, and Stevens's subsistence pledges were widely ignored. Most fishing passed to non-Native hands, overfishing and dams reduced fish stocks, and the state extended controls over fishing—including what Native fishing remained. It often seemed that the Stevens treaties had never been signed.

Yet the treaties were only dormant, and the civil rights movement of the 1960s created new horizons. Encouraged by the sit-ins of southern black Americans, Indians began "fish-ins" to protest restrictions on their treaty right to fish. Led by Puyallup activists Bob Satiacum and James Young, and the Nisqually's Billy Frank, Natives fished in their traditional ways and places, in violation of laws regulating gear and seasons. The fish-ins continued through the stormy 1960s, galvanizing Native identity across tribal lines—and sometimes ending in violence. In September 1970, protesters shot at wardens dismantling Indian nets, and demonstrators were teargassed and 60 arrested. Yet radicalism drew attention to the crusade, and nine days later President Nixon's Justice Department filed suit against Washington State for violating treaty rights.

Lightning struck on February 12, 1974, when—in the most contested legal decision in Washington state history—federal Judge George H. Boldt found against the state, affirming the Stevens treaties and ruling that half of the state's annual salmon catch belonged to Natives. Non-Native fishermen were up in arms, and violence flared again. The judge was burned in effigy and received death threats. But the Supreme Court upheld his decision in 1979, and later rulings extended it beyond salmon to other fish.

Boldt's verdict was no magic wand ensuring Native prosperity. Following federal passage in 1988 of a law permitting on-reservation gambling, many tribes turned to casinos to fill tribal coffers, albeit amid controversy and with mixed success. At any rate, for the first time since the Isaac Stevens era, Indians had something besides fish and land that non-Natives craved.

Boldt's ruling was a bitter pill for non-Native fishermen, who had families to support, too. Combined with the decline in salmon stocks, the decision forced a downsize of the non-Native fishing fleet. Yet the judgment put teeth in old promises and eventually all parties were more-or-less reconciled. Reminiscing in 2002, seventy-one-year-old Billy Frank acknowledged his one-time adversary, the state, for its help in tribal efforts to restore Nisqually Delta salmon habitat in the post-Boldt era. Salmon restoration was indeed the new dilemma for, as one expert on the controversy said, it does no good to secure treaty rights if there are no fish to be caught.

WPPSS!

The unfinished nuclear power site at Satsop, Washington.

"It costs too much. And we don't need it." By 1976, Seattle councilman John Miller's curt appraisal summarized the feelings of many Washingtonians about nuclear plants to generate electricity. Six years later, following revelations of mismanagement and mammoth cost overruns, the Washington Public Power Supply System defaulted on a bond obligation of $2.25 billion. The debt was amassed to build five nuclear plants and the default shifted a crushing repayment burden to customers. Small wonder the corporate acronym—WPPSS—became "whoops" in the ratepayer vocabulary.

WPPSS's beginnings in the 1950s seemed bright. Hydropower from Columbia River dams had accustomed northwesterners to cheap energy. People warmed their homes with electricity and stocked them with electric appliances. The aluminum industry born in World War II required low-cost power, and Northwest rates were the nation's lowest. Forecasters envisioned rising demand, predicting needs that might double every ten years. WPPSS arose in 1957 as an alliance of seventeen power companies and utility districts, whose managers came from the boards of its member utilities. They represented varied backgrounds—education, farming, small business—but lacked expertise in large public works or high finance.

The new alliance enjoyed municipality status, with the ability to float tax-free bonds to finance projects. It got off to an auspicious start in 1964, with the penny-wise completion of a $10.5 million hydroelectric plant at Packwood Lake in the Cascades, ahead of schedule. It also inaugurated a nuclear steam-generating plant at Hanford in 1966. The early '60s marked the high tide of enthusiasm regarding nuclear energy's peacetime uses. Authorities feared that dams could not meet electricity needs, and state and federal officials encouraged WPPSS to start down the nuclear path.

By 1972 the supply system had hatched plans for five nuclear power plants—two at Satsop and three at Hanford—with total costs reckoned at $4.1 billion. Yet designs kept changing as federal agencies imposed new safety requirements, and the state ruled that plants must be built by a variety of firms and subcontractors—not all of whom were reliable. Deficient work was torn apart and redone, while inflation pushed costs higher. Environmentalists intervened, exhorting the perils of nuclear generation. It became clear, as well, that prophecies of swelling electricity demand were overblown. Seattle City Light had already pulled out of the Plant 4 project at Hanford and the Plant 5 facility at Satsop in 1976, and WPPSS foundered. In 1984, it did launch Plant 2 at Hanford—today's Columbia Generating Station. But that was two years after costs estimated at $24 billion forced it to stop work on Plants 4 and 5, leaving ratepayers holding the bag. Lawsuits arising from the mess were finally settled in 1995, and neither ratepayers nor investors were happy. Plants 1 and 3 were also scrapped.

Thanks to eleventh-hour shuffles at the top, a downsized WPPSS survived the calamity, though it changed its name to Energy Northwest in 1998. Based in Richland, it operates the nuclear Columbia Generating Station. After years of inefficient operation, power from this upgraded Hanford facility became competitive in price. Periodic droughts and international crises arouse energy anxieties and prompt ideas of giving nuclear power a second look. Yet driving down State Route 8 in Grays Harbor County, nothing reminds the motorist more of Don Quixote's windmills than the abandoned 496-foot cooling towers of the unfinished Satsop reactors.

OF OWLS AND
OLD-GROWTH FORESTS

Loggers and giant cedar, 1906.

Early photographers like Darius Kinsey liked to group loggers around some old-growth monarch—a 1,000-year-old Douglas fir, a mammoth red cedar—with one man reclining in the undercut. The pose combined a folksy, "believe it or not" appeal with the idea of men as masters of nature. The eyes of most early Washingtonians were fixed on earning a living. Unacquainted with affluence as a norm, they gave little thought to posterity. But by the 1970s, Americans had enjoyed years of mass consumption. And most ancient forest was gone forever, replaced by urban sprawl, monoculture tree plantations, or regrowth timber in national forests. Yet the state still contained stands of old-growth trees older than 200 years. Environmentalists aimed to save what remained.

Ancient forests, they believed, are sanctuaries to cherish. Green forest canopies distill the air, and lichen-carpeted root systems filter ground water and stop erosion. Salmon need clean gravel to spawn, but clear-cutting and logging roads promote runoff that kills streams. Some threatened species, like the marbled murrelet or the northern spotted owl, cannot live without ancient trees. The spotted owl was scarcely known until 1968. Researchers then declared that over 2,000 pairs inhabited the Northwest, and it became the poster species for old forests. The owl nests in broken tops of ancient trees, and needs the canopy of biodiverse forest as a rain shield, since its feathers don't shed water. For environmentalists, it was a barometer whose survival monitored the health of fragile woodlands, signifying a new-era humility that viewed human needs as one mere part of nature's symbiosis.

The crusade produced some nasty conflicts with timber corporations, loggers, and sawmill workers. Since World War II, business and workers agreed on a conservationist approach that imagined nature as something to be managed to provide profits and jobs. "The timber harvest by which ye live takes many of the great, old, ripe trees," advised the script of a company-sponsored forest pageant. "If they were not taken, soon they would die, rot and fall." Logging trucks in small-town forest festivals of the '50s, their bumpers festooned with evergreen swags, paraded giant sections of old-growth trunks. But environmentalism made steady progress, using media and the courts to advance its goals. To an increasingly concerned public, clear-cuts began to look more like battlefield wastelands than sites for reforestation. A minority of activists adopted in-your-face tactics to save the forests. They staged tree sit-ins or drove spikes into trunks to discourage cutting, which might maim a worker if struck by a saw. The state was caught in between. It created a Department of Ecology in 1970, but owned two million acres of forests whose harvests supported public schools.

To forestall regulation of private lands, corporations adopted many environmentalist ideas. Yet they defended clear-cutting as crucial to the full sunlight needed for reforestation. In federal forests, however, the preservationists carried the day via publicity and legal process. Lumbering was once Washington's premier industry and forest products are still the state's third largest manufacturing sector. But the state's total harvest slipped 25 percent in the last two decades of the twentieth century, and the volume culled from federal land plunged more than 90 percent between 1980 and 1996, sending many sawmills and small loggers out of business. Lumbermen still craved old-growth timber for its mass and prime market quality, but little or no ancient wood was being felled in Washington's 800,000 acres of federally owned old-growth forest. Three-quarters of the harvest was coming from private lands that contained one-third of the state's timber.

THE GATES OF MICROSOFT

Bill Gates.

In Xanadu did Kubla Khan a stately pleasure dome decree. . . .

It somehow seemed right to invoke Coleridge's mysterious old poem "Kubla Khan," with its scent of oriental splendor and power. Xanadu references abounded in the 1990s, as reporters followed the progress of the Lake Washington pleasure dome being built by high-tech potentate Bill Gates. When the forty-one-year-old Gates and wife Melinda occupied the estate in 1997—with its trout stream, thirty-car garage, and reception hall for 100 guests—he'd spent $53 million. But then his personal worth was an estimated $36 billion ($90 billion by 1999). In 1994 *Fortune* had already named Gates the world's wealthiest person.

William H. Gates III was no stranger to comfort, even before he made his billions. His father was a Seattle lawyer and his mother a regent of the University of Washington. At Lakeside prep school he met Paul Allen, the future cofounder of his Microsoft Corporation. Computers were then rare, but Lakeside had a teletype link to one downtown. He and Allen got hooked. They began programming, devising a scheduling system for the school and a program to analyze traffic patterns.

In 1973 Gates went to Harvard, but Allen chanced upon a *Popular Electronics* story that changed their futures. It described a small machine, the Altair 8800, a primitive ancestor of the personal computer. Gates and Allen got the company's go-ahead to create an Altair computer language, derived from an existing code called BASIC. When it worked, Gates dropped out of Harvard and joined Allen in Albuquerque, where they founded Microsoft in 1975 to make software. In 1979 they moved their shop to Seattle's suburbs.

Microsoft's big score came in 1980, when IBM asked Gates to create an operating system for its new personal computer (PC), the desktop machine that would make microcomputers household items. With foxy finesse, Gates bought an existing system devised by Tim Patterson for $50,000. When modified, it became MS-DOS, the operating system used by most of the seventy million IBM PCs and IBM clones built in the '80s. In a canny move, Gates persuaded IBM to make its PC specifications public. He could then sell MS-DOS, which he still owned, to firms that supplied or copied the PC.

Working fifteen-hour days, seven days a week, Gates took only a few days' vacation between 1978 and 1984. Paul Allen left the firm in 1983 due to cancer (which he overcame), but Microsoft's swelling workforce comprised the best and brightest technical minds. They worked 75-hour weeks, but enjoyed stock options in the company, which went public in 1986. Ten thousand Microsoft staffers became millionaires.

A new operating system called Windows was wildly successful in the 1990s. It was sold as a package that included Microsoft's other applications, like its word processor and internet browser. This strategy induced cries of unfair competition by Microsoft's rivals, and President Clinton's Justice Department sued the firm for monopoly practices in 1998. Courts concluded that Gates had stepped over antitrust lines, but did not order Microsoft's breakup.

While pressing on with new projects, Gates embraced philanthropy. In 1999 he created the Bill and Melinda Gates Foundation, which became America's largest charitable trust overnight. With his spreading links to telecommunications and financial networks, Gates stood astride the globalization highway at the dawn of the twenty-first century. Whether posterity will remember Washington's (so far) greatest entrepreneur as a hero is anyone's guess. It's safe to say, though, that whoever presently tries to assess his impact on our era is apt to employ tools that he pioneered.

JAVA JIVE

A Starbucks Coffee Shop

Just as Washington's wine industry started its 1970s climb to fame, a second beverage stirred the Northwest imagination. Coffee, a wake-up brew that most Americans sipped for pennies from humble mugs, began its makeover into a pricey artifact of nuanced consumption. The transformation was the result of marketing, and at the wizardry's center was Brooklyn-born Howard Schultz and his company, Starbucks.

As a beverage, coffee originated centuries ago—perhaps in Ethiopia. Over time it inspired varied institutions, from the cafes of Vienna and Paris to the hip coffeehouses of America's '50s beat generation and '60s folk music scene. Its current gourmet vogue has California roots. In 1966, Dutch-born Alfred Peet opened a Berkeley roastery to sell superior arabica coffee beans rather than cheaper robusta beans that corporate brands used in grocery-store grinds. Then, in 1971, three Seattleites—Gordon Bowker, Jerry Baldwin, and Zev Siegl—began selling arabica beans in Pike Place Market. They named their shop Starbucks after a character in Melville's Moby Dick and designed a cute mermaid logo to complement the store's maritime decor. The trio didn't serve coffee by the cup, only whole beans for customers to grind. Peet was their supplier, and taught them art of roasting. They started roasting their own beans and expanded to four Seattle locations by 1981.

In that year Schultz visited the company, saw its promise, and convinced the partners to make him marketing director. Visiting

Milan in 1983, Schultz savored its array of espresso brews. An infusion of Italianate flair into Starbuck's business model, he guessed, might add a whiff of sophistication to Seattle's stores. He couldn't convert Starbuck's founders to his vision, so he opened his own espresso boutique. Crafting frothy lattes and cappuccinos, the store was a quick success. In 1987 he bought all of Starbucks's stores and its brand for $3.8 million.

Schultz went public in 1992; by 2008 Starbucks had 16,680 stores in 47 countries and 176,000 workers. It was an empire of company shops, licensees, and partnerships, more like McDonald's than Milan's espresso bars. Schultz worked his magic by selling superior coffee, inventing a raft of novelty beverages, and selling much else: food, music CDs—even instant coffee. He offered atmosphere too, touting Starbucks as a haven between work and home and its baristas as mentors in the espresso mystique. His sales strategy linked epicurean consumerism (with its in-crowd tasting vocabulary inspired by wine) to trending aspirations for world betterment: social justice, environmentalism, fair trade for coffee growers, and an honest deal for his employees—decent pay, health plans, stock options. Customers could feel virtuous while indulging their tastes.

The business became so big that it aroused backlash. In 1999, mobs ransacked Seattle stores while protesting multi-national corporatism during a World Trade Organization meeting. Cynics complained that Starbucks used non-recyclable cups, that its water bottles created plastic waste, that its compassion was glib and profit-driven. There were protests over Schultz's refusal to unionize. Basketball fans fumed when Schultz, who bought Seattle's Supersonics team in 2001, sold it to moguls who moved it to Oklahoma in 2008. The company's success encouraged competitors; even McDonalds introduced a high-end cup of joe (Schultz was caught off-guard when Consumer Reports declared it better than his own brew). Then Starbucks's expansion was momentarily stalled by the recession of 2008–09.

Yet the company navigated such storms. Amidst renewed growth, java's impresario opened ornate "Roastery stores" in Seattle's Capitol Hill (2014) and Shanghai (2017) to showcase the "theatre of coffee." In 2018, he launched another campaign, unveiling a "Reserve store" in Seattle's SoDo district, the prototype for possibly 1,000 shops dispensing cocktails to "introduce America to Italian aperitivo culture."

Amazon's Empire

The Amazon Spheres in Seattle.

In 2018, Amazon unveiled a cluster of three gleaming domes on downtown Seattle's north side. "The Spheres"—a monument to Amazon-founder Jeff Bezos's e-commerce, media, and technology empire—may one day rival the Space Needle as a city symbol. Climate-controlled, teeming with tropical plants, the structure was conceived as a creative oasis for select members of the company's Seattle-area staff of 45,000—the city's largest workforce.

Amazon's rise since the mid-1990s was meteoric. Born in Albuquerque and raised in Texas and Florida, Bezos displayed can-do energy from childhood. Graduating from Princeton in 1986, he worked several years on Wall Street. Yet he envisioned an entrepreneurial career. In New York, he encountered the idea that the emerging internet web might become a global marketplace—an "everything store." Books, he surmised, would be a smart place to start. Portable for easy mail-order internet sale, they were readily obtained from existing distributors.

For his headquarters Bezos chose Seattle. With Microsoft there, and the University of Washington, it had high-tech talent to build marketing and distribution software. And Washington was small, population-wise—a blessing since court rulings held that online firms need only collect sales taxes in states where they physically operated. Outside Washington, Amazon could pass those savings on to customers, underselling traditional bookstores. (Under pressure from the states, Amazon eventually began collecting taxes, but by then it had a mammoth jump on brick-and-mortar merchants.)

Bezos began in his Bellevue garage, with his own savings and $100,000 from his parents. He named his company Amazon after the world's greatest river, with its aura of unstoppable mass and momentum. Amazon.com recorded its maiden sales in mid-1995 and, with deep-discount prices, it soared. Skeptics thought customers wouldn't entrust their credit cards to the Web, but enticed by unbeatable prices, unlimited choice, and one-click convenience, millions raced to do so. Bezos demanded a corporate culture of frugality and super-aggressive growth. Helping ignite the dot-com investment fever of the late 1990s, he took the company public in 1997. He operated at losses, deferring dividends and reinvesting earnings to hire talent, build software, and leverage deals. Keeping the pedal on full-stop growth, he outstripped other start-ups and narrowly survived when the speculative bubble burst, in 2000–01.

Amazon snared customers by personalizing their shopping. When J. K. Rowling's fourth Harry Potter novel appeared, he slashed its price 40 percent and guaranteed release-day, front-door delivery for no extra charge. Amazon lost serious money but earned loyalty from millions of Rowling's fans. Readers were enthralled by technology that let them browse select passages from books online. Amazon's Kindle electronic-book reader popularized instantly downloadable ebooks. With the Amazon Prime program, Bezos created a buyer's club with free two-day shipping. Along the way, he extended his Faustian grasp to products as far-flung as diapers and cloud-computing services.

A fierce and relentless innovator, Bezos personified economist Josef Schumpeter's idea of "creative destruction" via new methods of capitalist wealth creation. His success made casualties of small retailers, chain stores, and shopping malls; to be "Amazoned" meant out-innovated, undersold, and perhaps ruined. When Bezos bought the Whole Foods food chain for $13.5 billion in 2017, he ignited "Amazon paranoia" among giants in the grocery trade. In 2013, he established an elephant-sized media footprint by buying the Washington Post. Even earlier, his imagination vaulted beyond earth, with the 2003 creation of his Blue Origin space-exploration project. In 2018, just as the glittering Spheres were opened, Amazon surpassed its Seattle neighbor Microsoft in stock market valuation, and the Seattle Times pronounced Bezos the planet's richest person.

BRAVE NEW WORLD

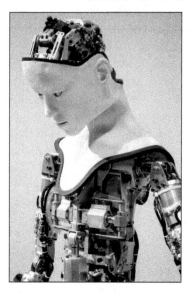

". . .there is nothing new under the sun."

In our age of breathtaking innovation, as marketing grooms us for the next cool thing, folks may doubt this claim by the sage of Ecclesiastes. Consider, though, another of his notions: *". . .in much wisdom is much grief, and he who increases knowledge increases sorrow."* In today's sprint to create and monetize "artificial intelligence" (AI)—to build and profit from machines that think, speak, and act like humans—are we paving a path to U- or Dystopia, or perhaps some of both? A wealth of fable and fiction, from mythology's Prometheus to Kubrick's 2001, extends the biblical warning. Twentieth-century ideology and warfare, too, with their record of science gone awry, loom as signposts of reason's sometime inability or unwillingness to control its inventions wisely.

After 1980, metro-Seattle burgeoned as an academic-entrepreneurial complex, a hub of AI research and its applications. A technology rush now transforms the region's markets and values—more than gold changed them around 1900. At the revolution's hinge is Microsoft co-founder Paul Allen. When Allen and Bill Gates moved Microsoft from Albuquerque to Washington in 1979, Seattle was in the doldrums. With its dazzling success, Microsoft became the fulcrum for resurgence, a magnet for brain power and venture-capitalist start-ups—most dramatically, Amazon. Aided by Microsoft's philanthropy, the University of Washington's advanced AI program surged to the nation's top five. Its graduates moved freely within a knowledge-growth and wealth-creation ecosystem.

In 2003, Allen founded the Allen Institute for Brain Science, to map the brain. In 2014, he established its sibling Allen Institute for

Artificial Intelligence and hired Oren Etzioni, a UW professor, to direct it. (His Vulcan corporation also acquired sixty acres east of the Monorail, selling much of it to Amazon to build its corporate campus between 2014 and 2018.) Allen aimed to supersede machines that could beat humans at chess—as impressive as such feats were. He wanted programs with humanlike "common sense," inferential logic, and contextual vision, mimicking the real-world savvy children evolve as they learn by trial and error. His team started by designing programs to pass grade-school science exams. Their goal was a program that not only answered correctly, but justified its answers at grade-twelve level. Yet building truly self-aware machines, Allen thought, might take a century.

Allen and Etzioni were AI optimists; they stressed its pursuit "for the common good," though they acknowledged the ethical quandaries surrounding robotics. On the pessimistic side, physicist Stephen Hawking warned it might spell the "end of the human race." In 2017, Etzioni responded in the New York Times. The risks are real, he conceded, but once the horse has escaped the barn, we have no pragmatic option. AI is already a tool of geopolitics; if we don't embrace it, others will surpass us. But we must regulate it, and he proposed guidelines to refine ideas advanced by Isaac Asimov in 1942: AI systems must 1) respect all laws that govern their human operators; 2) disclose that they are not human; and 3) respect the norms of privacy. Etzioni admitted that his rules were broad discussion starters, but it's hard to dispute his point about the horse and barn. Yet Hawking's long-term fears resonate: AI might "take off on its own, and re-design itself at an ever-increasing rate. Humans, who are limited by slow biological evolution, couldn't compete, and would be superseded." In that case, not everyone will be consoled by Asimov's 1972 suggestion: "How could we consummate the victory of intelligence over nature more gloriously than by passing on our heritage, in triumph, to a greater intelligence—of our own making." In the short term, it's clear that the rush to profit from prosthetic intelligence (errant self-driving cars, enhanced surveillance, and massive breaches of privacy) will yield serious malfunctions. Time will tell if Puget Sound's AI culture (and the world's) can or will nurture safeguards to control, as much as advance it.

TOWARD THE FUTURE

Space Needle and monorail, 1962.

"How can our state grow with grace?" It was a thorny question posed with elegance by Washington Governor Dan Evans in 1966. At one time, growth had not caused concern. Salmon seemed inexhaustible in the 1870s. As for forests, John Muir said in 1888 that Puget Sound settlers considered trees "their greatest enemies—a sort of larger pernicious weed immensely difficult to get rid of." Around 1900 Spokane was lord of the "Inland Empire," and a promotion for Tacoma pictured a skyline of smelters belching soot.

For the first two centuries of its modern history, Washington was imagined in terms of growth, fueled by natural abundance: furs, soil, gold, coal, fish, timber, and water. The Depression, World War II, and the Cold War, with their welfare and defense projects, propelled the state to modernity. The 1962 World's Fair in Seattle, with its Space Needle and monorail, imagined a stellar role for Washington on the interstellar horizon. Spokane's World's Fair in 1974 echoed the optimism—though its motto, "Progress without Pollution," had a tinge of sobriety.

Having arrived at the cusp of history and industry, some pondered

Washington's regional character and texture of life. Limits to growth came into vogue. In the 1970s, two fantasies materialized at extreme corners of the regional imagination: the nightmare of Pugetopolis, a reflection of the Northeast's megalopolis; and the reverie of Ecotopia, a utopia of pristine nature saved from urban blight.

The Microsoft revolution carried Washington to new heights in the 1980s and 1990s, but the dot-com bust after 2000 was a sobering comedown. Looking back, it's instructive to remember that Alweg, the Swiss builder of Seattle's monorail in 1962, hailed its space-age version of the elevated train as "the first practical demonstration of monorail as mass rapid transit in an urban area." Forty years later some Seattleites revived the forgotten notion of constructing a regional monorail network. In the interim, the Alweg monorail had been shortened a block due to downtown renewal. And meanwhile, Seattle and King County were suffering one of the nation's worst traffic problems.

Yet two statements—one by photographer Asahel Curtis, one by Senator Scoop Jackson—merit reflection. Curtis straddled the line between commercialism and conservation. He loved wild places, helped found The Mountaineers, and was chairman of the Mount Rainier National Park Committee. On the question of highways and mass use of the park, already controversial in the 1930s, Curtis wrote: "I realize that the true Mountaineer would much rather see the mountains from the trail or unexplored wilderness, but . . . to get the majority of people into them, it is necessary to have roads." Senator Jackson, who won the Sierra Club's John Muir Award for conservation, also insisted on balance: "It's fine for the people who have made it to say we won't have any more economic growth," he observed. "How about the six million at the [national] poverty level? We have an obligation to them."

Washington's first non-Indian visitors thought of the region as a promised land. Perhaps, in their fashion, its Native Indians thought of it that way too, before the settlers arrived. Promised lands are myths, but potent ones. The thoughts of African-American author Esther Hall Mumford perhaps ring true for many of her fellow Washingtonians, whatever their ethnicity: "For African American people," Mumford wrote, "Washington has been an imperfect Promised Land. But to paraphrase a 1923 Seattle migrant, Bertha Pitts Campbell, it was, and still is, 'a good place to start something'."

POSTSCRIPT, 2018:
A TIME OF CHANGE

Washingtonians once called their state America's "fourth corner"—often with some pride. The subtitle of *Washington's History*, created for its 2003 edition, calls it the "far Northwest." These terms may suggest a place remote from the center. Lewis and Clark certainly imagined it that way, though the Native American peoples they encountered surely did not. The discovery of Yukon gold in the 1890s brought focus to Puget Sound as a trailhead for the gold rush, which thrust Washington from the frontier to the modern era. Yet as late as the 1960s and 1970s, an aim of Seattle's and Spokane's World Fairs was to put Washington on the map—to show people elsewhere that it was not someplace you had to leave to "make it big." In the scant forty years since Microsoft settled in Washington, the state has been transformed in important ways. Now, economist Enrico Moretti calls Puget Sound "one of the world's pre-eminent innovation hubs." The soil, orchards, and vineyards of the Columbia watershed yield crops relished around the world. The likes of Gates, Allen, Schultz, or Bezos would surely agree that Washington is—as Bertha Pitts Campbell said in 1923—"a good place to start something."

In 2003, this book stressed the state's rise to a "front-and-center spot" in world affairs, but in 2018 the trajectory of its continuing ascent is even steeper and faster. Change is perhaps the only constant of history, but what's often vital for its human impact is its tempo. In the past decade-and-a-half, the rate of regional change has accelerated. Fifteen years ago, the e-commerce revolution's initial burst had just fizzled in the dot-com stock market bust of 2000–01, and it wasn't clear that Amazon's business model would reshape world trade and technology as it has. Nor had the force of the digital world's automation dynamic, fueled by machine learning and artificial intelligence research, become so clear.

Today's Washington is a great place to begin something, but new starts can spawn challenging outcomes and discontents—a cardinal fact of modern revolutions. Depending on one's generational cohort, social station and point of view, escalating change makes some things seem better, others shocking, unwelcome, or intractable. The

"Cascade curtain"—the cultural divide between eastern and western Washington (the east mainly rural, agricultural and "conservative," the west more urbanized and "progressive")—has perhaps risen taller (though the high-tech revolution inevitably spreads to agribusiness). Group-think ideological labels like "right" and "left," "progressive" and "conservative," get in the way of good sense. Drivers negotiating swelling traffic and strip-mall congestion between the Canadian and Oregon borders--especially on Interstate 5's Everett-Seattle-Tacoma axis—do not sing praises to progress. Between the two futuristic visions of the 1970s previously cited—sprawling urban overfill and nature saved from blight—the scales tip toward the former. Rising costs in western Washington force some people into grueling commutes, pushing Pugetopolis farther north and south along the I-5 ribbon. Ugly confrontations, sometimes laced with hyperbolic charges of "racism" and "elitism," divide urbanites over planning policies, even in some smaller towns. "Never in my furthest imagination could I believe that a local issue like this could pit a community against itself in this manner," lamented one Bellingham resident in a recent public hearing on planning issues. One ponders Edmund Coleman's happy 1868 dream, cited in this book's prologue, of "busy multitudes" on the shores of Bellingham Bay.

In 2017 Amazon declared its intent to establish a second North American headquarters beyond Seattle, promising some new city billions in investment and 50,000 top-paying jobs. Scores of cities scrambled to submit bids, offering dramatic tax concessions and enticements. In a *New York Times* commentary, nationally-respected journalist Timothy Egan, a Seattle native, cautioned the contestants to mind their wishes. "What comes with the title of being the fastest growing big city in the country, with having the nation's hottest real estate market, is that the city no longer works for some people. For many others, the pace of change, not to mention the traffic, has been disorienting. The character of Seattle, a rain-loving communal shrug, has changed. Now we're a city on amphetamines." Amphetamines chased with espresso shots, he might have added. Washington today, in many ways, stands at the center things. Making the center hold will be a challenge.

Bibliography

Ambrose, Stephen E. *Undaunted Courage: Meriwether Lewis, Thomas Jefferson, and the Opening of the West.* New York: Simon and Schuster, 1996.

Asimov, Isaac. *Asimov's Guide to Science.* New York: Basic Books, 1972.

Beckham, Stephen Dow. *Lewis and Clark: From the Rockies to the Pacific.* Portland. Ore.: Graphic Arts Center Publishing, 2002.

Bergon, Frank, ed. *The Journals of Lewis and Clark.* New York: Penguin Books, 1989.

Boxberger, Daniel L. *To Fish in Common: The Ethnohistory of the Lummi Indian Salmon Fishery.* Seattle: University of Washington Press, 2000.

Brandt, Richard L. *One Click: Jeff Bezos and the Rise of Amazon.* New York: Portfolio/Penguin, 2012

Brewster, David, and David M. Buerge. *Washingtonians: A Biographical Portrait of the State.* Seattle: Sasquatch Books, 1988.

Bussing-Burks, Marie. *Starbucks.* Santa Barbara, CA: Greenwood Press, 2009

Chatters, James C. *Ancient Encounters: Kennewick Man and the First Americans.* New York: Simon and Schuster, 2001.

Clark, Norman H. *Washington: A Bicentennial History.* New York: W. W. Norton, 1976.

Coleman, Edmund T. "Mountaineering on the Pacific." *Harper's Magazine,* 39 (Nov. 1869): 793-817.

Cook, Warren. *Flood Tide of Empire: Spain and the Pacific Northwest, 1543-1819.* New Haven: Yale University Press, 1973.

Dietrich, William. *Northwest Passage: The Great Columbia River.* Seattle: University of Washington Press, 1995.

Downey, Roger. *Riddle of the Bones: Politics, Science, Race, and the Story of Kennewick Man.* New York: Copernicus Books, 2000.

Drucker, Philip. *Indians of the Northwest Coast.* Garden City: Natural History Press, 1963.

Eaton, Diane, and Sheila Urbanek. *Paul Kane's Great Nor-West.* Vancouver: University of British Columbia Press, 1995.

Edwards, G. Thomas, and Carlos A. Schwantes, eds. *Experiences in a Promised Land: Essays in Pacific Northwest History.* Seattle:

University of Washington Press, 1986.

Ficken, Robert E. *Washington Territory*. Pullman: Washington State University Press, 2002.

Ficken, Robert E., and Charles P. Le Warne. *Washington: A Centennial History*. Seattle: University of Washington Press, 1988.

Friday, Chris. *Organizing Asian American Labor: The Pacific Coast Canned-Salmon Industry, 1870-1942*. Philadelphia: Temple University Press, 1994.

Furtwangler, Albert. *Answering Chief Seattle*. Seattle: University of Washington Press, 1997.

Gibson, James R. *Otter Skins, Boston Ships, and China Goods: The Maritime Fur Trade of the Northwest Coast, 1785-1841*. Seattle: University of Washington Press, 1992.

Gough, Barry M. *The Northwest Coast: British Navigation, Trade, and Discoveries to 1812*. Vancouver: University of British Columbia Press, 1992.

Hayes, Derek. *Historical Atlas of the Pacific Northwest*. Seattle: Sasquatch Books, 1999.

Holm, Bill. *Northwest Coast Indian Art: An Analysis of Form*. Seattle: University of Washington Press, 1965.

Irvine, Ronald, with Walter J. Clore. *The Wine Project: Washington State's Winemaking History*. Vashon, Wash.: Sketch Publications, 1997.

Jarvela, Andrea. *The Washington Almanac*. Portland, Ore.: WestWinds Press, 1999.

Johansen, Dorothy O., and Charles M. Gates. *Empire of the Columbia: A History of the Pacific Northwest*. 2d ed. New York: Harper and Row, 1967.

Kirk, Ruth, and Carmela Alexander. *Exploring Washington's Past: A Road Guide to History*. Seattle: University of Washington Press, 1990.

Kruckeberg, Arthur R. *The Natural History of the Puget Sound Country*. Seattle: University of Washington Press, 1991.

Lee, W. Storrs, ed. *Washington State: A Literary Chronicle*. New York: Funk and Wagnalls, 1969.

Miller, Gary K. *Energy Northwest: A History of the Washington Public Power Supply System*. Richland: Energy Northwest, 2001.

Millner, Darrell. "George Bush of Tumwater: Founder of the First American Colony on Puget Sound." *Columbia*, 8 (Winter 1994/95): 14-19.

Moretti, Enrico. *The New Geography of Jobs*. Boston: Houghton Mifflin Harcourt, 2012

Morgan, Lane. *Greetings from Washington: A Glimpse at the Past Through Postcards*. Portland, Ore.: Graphic Arts Center Publishing, 1988.

Morgan, Murray. *Skid Road: An Informal Portrait of Seattle*. New York: Ballantine Books, 1971.

Murray, Keith. *The Pig War*. Tacoma: Washington State Historical Society, 1968.

Nisbet, Jack. *Singing Grass, Burning Sage: Discovering Washington's Shrub-Steppe*. Portland, Ore.: Graphic Arts Center Publishing, 1999.

Radke, August Carl. *Pacific American Fisheries, Inc.: A History of a Washington State Salmon Packing Company, 1890-1966*. Jefferson, N.C.: McFarland, 2002.

Richards, Kent D. *Isaac I. Stevens: Young Man in a Hurry*. Provo: Brigham Young University Press, 1979.

Ruzich, Constance M., "For the Love of Joe: The Language of Starbucks," *The Journal of Popular Culture*, 41, No. 3 (2008): 428-441

Saling, Ann. *The Great Northwest Nature Fact Book*. Rev. ed. Portland, Ore.: WestWinds Press, 1999.

Schwantes, Carlos Antonio. *The Pacific Northwest: An Interpretive History*. Rev. ed. Lincoln: University of Nebraska Press, 1996.

Scott, James W., and Roland L. De Lorme. *Historical Atlas of Washington*. Norman: University of Oklahoma Press, 1988.

Stone, Brad. *The Everything Store: Jeff Bezos and the Age of Amazon*. New York: Little, Brown and Co., 2013

Stratton, David H., ed. *Washington Comes of Age: The State in the National Experience*. Pullman: Washington State University Press, 1992.

Thomas, David Hurst. *Skull Wars: Kennewick Man, Archaeology, and the Battle for Native American Identity*. New York: Basic Books, 2000.

Vouri, Michael. *The Pig War*. Friday Harbor, Wash.: Griffen Bay
    Bookstore, 1999.

Warren, James R. *The War Years: A Chronicle of Washington State
    in World War II*. Seattle: History Ink, 2000.

White, Sid, and S. E. Solberg. *Peoples of Washington: Perspectives
    on Cultural Diversity*. Pullman: Washington State University
    Press, 1989.

Winthur, Oscar Osburn. *The Great Northwest: A History*. 2d ed.
    New York: Alfred A. Knopf, 1960.

Index

Photo Credits

Page 2: Bureau of Reclamation.
5: Dresser Project, Whatcom Museum of History and Art, Bellingham, Washington. **8:** #679, J. W. Sandison Collection, Whatcom Museum of History and Art, Bellingham, Washington. **14:** Special Collections, Wilson Library, Western Washington University, Bellingham, Washington. **16:** #7435, Whatcom Museum of History and Art, Bellingham, Washington. **18:** Northwest Room, Spokane Public Library. **20:** MSCUA, University of Washington Libraries, Negative no: NA 1972. **22:** Northwest Museum of Arts and Culture, Spokane; Photo by author. **24:** MSCUA, University of Washington Libraries, Negative no: NA 740. **26:** MSCUA, University of Washington Libraries, Negative no: NA 3992. **28:** Special Collections, Wilson Library, Western Washington University, Bellingham, Washington. **30:** Museo de América, Madrid. **32:** Special Collections, Wilson Library, Western Washington University, Bellingham, Washington (both). **34:** Special Collections, Wilson Library, Western Washington University, Bellingham, Washington. **36:** National Park Service, Independence National Historical Park, Philadelphia. **38:** Special Collections, Wilson Library, Western Washington University, Bellingham, Washington. **40:** U.S. Library of Congress. **42:** National Archives of Canada, C-008711. **44:** MSCUA, University of Washington Libraries, Negative no: NA 4171. **46:** MSCUA, University of Washington Libraries,

Negative no: NA 4166. **48:** Special Collections, Wilson Library, Western Washington University, Bellingham, Washington. **50:** Missouri Historical Society, St. Louis, entry of ca. 30 January 1806, Clark Family Collection, William Clark Papers. **52:** Jesuit Oregon Province Archives, Gonzaga University, Negative no: 802.21a. **54:** 1996.10.3248, Whatcom Museum of History and Art, Bellingham, Washington. **56:** San Juan Island NHP. **58:** 83.10.6331, Museum of History and Industry, Seattle. **60:** MSCUA, University of Washington Libraries, Negative no: UW 22024; Special Collections, Wilson Library, Western Washington University, Bellingham, Washington. **62:** Chief Seattle, SHS67, Museum of History and Industry, Seattle; Henry Smith, MSCUA, University of Washington Libraries, Negative no: A. Curtis 5895, Asahel Curtis Coll. 482. **64:** Photo collection of the State Capitol Museum, Washington State Historical Society, Tacoma. **66:** Washington State Historical Society, Tacoma, Curtis photo, Neg. 21809. **68:** San Juan Island NHP. **70:** Image #1780, Courtesy of the Renton Historical Society, Renton. **72:** MSCUA, University of Washington Libraries, Negative no: A. Curtis 33545, Asahel Curtis Photo Co. Collection no. 482. **74:** The Wing Luke Asian Museum, Seattle, Chin Chun Hock Wa Chong Co., Print COHP 12. **76:** 83.10.10135, Museum of History and Industry, Seattle. **78:** Courtesy of the Bancroft Library, University of California,

Berkeley, 1969.026-PIC. **80:** Courtesy Louis W. Hill Papers, James J. Hill Library, Saint Paul. **82:** postcard from *Lane Morgan's Greetings from Washington.* **84:** Northwest Museum of Arts and Culture, Spokane. **86:** #1996.10.864, Whatcom Museum of History and Art, Bellingham, Washington. **88:** #7380, Whatcom Museum of History and Art, Bellingham, Washington. **90:** Washington State Historical Society, Tacoma. **92:** #10283 _, D. Kinsey Collection, Whatcom Museum of History and Art, Bellingham, Washington. **94:** #1979.5.6, Whatcom Museum of History and Art, Bellingham, Washington. **95:** Washington State Historical Society, Tacoma, Negative no: EPH/796.93/ED21W 1936. **96:** MSCUA, University of Washington Libraries, Negative no: A. Curtis, 26368. **98:** Edward— Edward S. Curtis Gallery, McCloud, CA; Asahel—Washington State Historical Society, Negative no: 7515. **100:** Bureau of Reclamation. **102:** Courtesy of Bancroft Library, University of California, Berkeley, 19xx.334-A. **104:** SHS 12544, Museum of History and Industry, Seattle. **106:** 83.10.17698.2, Museum of History and Industry, Seattle. **108:** MSCUA, University of Washington Libraries, Negative no: UW 22025; Bartholick Collection,

Center for Pacific Northwest Studies, Western Washington University, Bellingham, Washington 98225-9123. **110:** PI-22145, Museum of History and Industry, Seattle. **112:** PI-28297, Museum of History and Industry, Seattle. **114:** #1985.21.3, Whatcom Museum of History and Art, Bellingham, Washington. **116:** HD.4 A.130, U. S. Department of Energy. **118:** Collection of the Supreme Court of the United States, Photograph number: 1939.182.2. **120:** Royal Ontario Museum. **122:** MSCUA, University of Washington Libraries, Negative no: UW 19599. **124:** Northwest Museum of Arts and Culture, Spokane. **126:** Courtesy of Energy Northwest. **128:** #20152, Whatcom Museum of History and Art, Bellingham, Washington. **130:** Courtesy of Microsoft Corporation. **132:** By SilentDeath [CC BY-SA 4.0], from Wikimedia Commons. **134:** By SounderBruce [CC BY-SA 4.0], from Wikimedia Commons. **136:** Photo by Franck V. on Unsplash. **138:** MSCUA, University of Washington Libraries, Negative no: UW 856.

About the Author

Harry Ritter is Emeritus Professor of History at Western Washington University, where he taught from 1969 to 2010. Born in St. Louis, Missouri, he received his doctorate in history from the University of Virginia. He is also the author of *Alaska's History: The People, Land, and Events of the North Country*. He lives in Bellingham, Washington.

Printed in the USA
CPSIA information can be obtained
at www.ICGtesting.com
JSHW012035140824
68134JS00033B/3077

9 781513 261690